MW00772862

THE
SYSTEMS
MINDSET

THE
SYSTEMS
MINDSET

MANAGING THE MACHINERY
OF YOUR LIFE

SAM CARPENTER

GREENLEAF
BOOK GROUP PRESS

Published by Greenleaf Book Group Press
Austin, Texas
www.gbgpress.com

Distributed by Greenleaf Book Group and North Sister Publishing

For ordering information, please contact Greenleaf Book Group LLC at PO Box 91869, Austin, TX 78709, 512.891.6100. For foreign rights information or special discounts for bulk purchases, contact North Sister Publishing, 141 NW Greenwood Ave., Suite 200, Bend, Oregon, 800.664.7448.

Design and composition by Greenleaf Book Group and Kim Lance
Cover design by Greenleaf Book Group and Kim Lance
Cover photo is Asima Sefic, 17, who is native to the city of Bihac, Bosnia and Herzegovina. Photographer Maja Topcagic is a freelance photographer based in Sarajevo, Bosnia and Herzegovina.

Cataloging-in-Publication data is available.

Print ISBN: 978-1-62634-252-1

eBook ISBN: 978-1-62634-253-8

16 17 18 19 20 21   10 9 8 7 6 5 4 3 2 1

First Edition

Also by Sam Carpenter

Work the System:
The Simple Mechanics of Making More and Working Less

In memory of my mother, Nancy Fox.

She told me not to write a book until I had
something useful to say.

"Keep your eyes on the road; your hands upon the wheel."

–JIM MORRISON, THE DOORS

CONTENTS

PREFACE

I've written *The Systems Mindset* to convince you to take a more mechanical approach to controlling your day's sights, sounds, and events. In making this transition and subsequently watching the physical aspects of your world dramatically improve, you'll find that the softer, emotional life realms get better, too.

Much better.

I want to show you that we live in a mechanical world and remind you that physical reality operates in the same way, everywhere, all the time. From this, I'll describe a simple life posture, one that will advance every area of your life.

And I am betting that through this different way of looking at your world, you'll become amazed again—the way you were when you were three years old.

An opaque veil will lift, making life vivid and understandable.

The genesis of *The Systems Mindset* stretches back to 2006, even before I began writing my business book, *Work the System: The Simple Mechanics of Making More and Working Less*, first published in 2008. *Work* and *Mindset* share precisely the same thread: that you can take control of your life if you view the world as it really is—a collection of superbly efficient independent systems—rather than what it isn't—a complex mass of discordant happenings.

Upon taking *Work* through three editions, I found that what had been most important to me all along—this different vision of how the world mechanically functions—was indeed what was

xiv THE SYSTEMS MINDSET

most important to my readers. So, with enthusiasm, I've written this explanation of the Systems Mindset without the business-book encumbrances of documentation and chessboard-strategy detail.

This guidebook is especially suited for anyone who doesn't own a business, who has a job, is a student, is a parent, or is retired. And it's for those who have little as well as for those of wealth.

It's written to take you to a new place in your life.

Mindset is relatively short, slightly less than half the size of *Work*. It's been easy to write because it's forged on real-life applications and successes. And success hasn't been mine alone. It's been the outcome for tens of thousands of others who have adopted the Systems Mindset and who have been able to more precisely make their lives what they want them to be.

Yes, I believe these concepts utterly.

What is the overarching message of these pages? If I had to condense it to one sentence, I'd say that managing your life effectively—and getting it to be the way you want it to be—is not a difficult thing to accomplish once the simple mechanics of life are grasped.

If you wish for further information on the systems mindset, see our online product, "A Course in the Systems Mindset." Go to thesystemsmindset.com/course.

Unusual in the literary world, I have a special relationship with my publisher, Greenleaf Book Group, in which I've kept ownership of my manuscripts. While, with my approval, Greenleaf oversees the editing, design, and production and gets my books into bookstores and other channels, I'm also able to distribute them myself.

Yes, it's about control.

The Systems Mindset has been in my head for a long time. It's good to finally get it down.

—Sam Carpenter,
February 2016

INTRODUCTION

You want control of your life.

Most people don't master this skill, so they struggle. In these pages I want to convince you that your existence is not an endless stream of erratic occurrences. Rather, it's a finite collection of logical, individual systems that are constantly at work producing the ongoing results of your life. This elementary yet profound insight will arrive suddenly, at a specific moment in time, and then it will be with you always. I call this epiphany "getting it."

I want to show you exactly how to manage the systems—the machinery—of your life: at home, at work, with your health, and in your relationships.

There's nothing mystical here. It will make complete sense, and it's all rooted in how the simple mechanics of the world physically function. It's in the physics of it all—the reality of up and down and back and forth, of movement, of breathing, of gravity, and of the same actions leading to the same results. It's about the nuts and bolts of our world that we can depend upon to operate the same way in every instance.

But it's my bet you haven't gone down this particular road before.

To take charge of your life, don't adopt a feel-good blanket theory that promises to contrive the life conditions you desire. Instead, get rooted in the physical, to see and then direct your results-producing machinery so you can generate the life conditions you desire.

And what about this machinery? Know that it's working 24/7, creating your life's results whether you know it or not, whether you like it or not, and whether you manage it or not.

And this is not a matter of "you control the machinery or the machinery will control you." It's more this: "You control the machinery or the machinery will produce random results that, as you continually attempt to sort out the chaos, will make your life a struggle."

The focus will be on what I call the Systems Mindset, the key stance in effectively managing everyday reality. I'll describe how this posture naturally morphs into the concept of System Improvement.

It's a good time to list some of my preferred synonyms for "system." I like process, protocol, machine, machinery, mechanism, and mechanics. I'll also point out here that some systems are visible (mechanical, touchable), while others are invisible (communication protocols for instance).

As I said, there's no mystery here, so let's get down to it. If you really "get" the following five points, you'll be on your way to managing the machinery of your life. The logic is so absurdly simple that nearly everyone overlooks it:

1. In this moment, every single result and condition of your life has been preceded by a simple step-by-step linear system (or process, protocol, or mechanism), and every single result and condition in your future will also be preceded by one of these simple step-by-step linear systems.

2. To get the life results you want, you must assertively manage these processes. Since most of them are recurring, you can improve them in the here and now so that when

they execute again in the future they'll produce optimal results.

3. Your personal attributes will not deliver you what you want in your life. They can help, of course, but they won't be directly responsible for your success. What matters is the machinery you create and maintain—and that machinery doesn't give a whit about your personal qualities.

4. The world is not a mess! It's an astonishingly organized place, with 99.9 percent of everything working just fine.

5. Spiritual transcendence (amazement) lies in the mechanical details of the right here, right now. It's not "out there" somewhere.

And these points beg the question: If you could see the individual systems of your life from moment to moment, would you assertively work to manage them so they produce the personal control you want?

(As an aside, does pursuing personal control sound selfish? Then consider the opposite: Is it somehow altruistic to allow chaos to reign?)

In employing the Systems Mindset to seize control of your life, you're not going to play mind games with yourself or violate somebody's rights or take anything away from anyone. On the contrary, intensively attending to your systems and gaining life control will lift up those around you. Why? Because by your example—and by the sheer value you will cause—you'll be opening up lines of life control for them, too.

Will your personality change? Yes, some. You'll still be you, but your level of personal confidence will skyrocket and you will be considerably more upbeat. You'll notice it, and the people around you will notice it, too. They'll wonder what's up as they watch your new vibrancy.

Arriving at this place takes little effort and it doesn't take much time.

To gain this level of control there's no need for blind faith or some kind of guru worship. And you don't have to forsake your current beliefs or walk away from what is important to you. The key to effectively managing your life doesn't lie outside you. It's inside, a straightforward construct that only requires a tweak in how you perceive your world. Make this elementary adjustment in how you see things and you will not only be able to determine your life's results, you'll watch each day unfold as a graceful, exhilarating dance. You'll discover that the magic you've been seeking all along is in life, just as it is.

In gaining firm control of things, will you become permanently happy? No, of course not. Although the road bumps will decrease significantly, they will still materialize now and then. But for sure, the ones that appear will be easier to negotiate when you're strong, resilient, and calm.

Your mounting personal potency will be a consequence of your new, crystal-clear understanding of how the machinery of life works.

Seventeen years ago, with the business I still own today, I had a flash of insight and then transformed my eighty-hour workweeks to just two hours. And at the same time I moved from impoverishment to wealth. What else happened? I rejuvenated my physical self, transitioning from a death spiral to the robust health I enjoy today. And what about my relationships? I went from zero personal connections to having welcoming friends all over the world.

I've moved from a chaotic, unpredictable existence to controlling the machinery of my life, and I want you to do the same.

Care to give it a shot?

—

Mindset is a guidebook, so I'll approach the principles from different angles and there will be some repetition just to embed the concepts. Yet within the first half-dozen chapters you'll realize that with your management, the machines of your life are going to come under your firm control and they're going to produce the results you desire.

I've written Part One in a Q&A, conversational format, as if I were teaching a class, so the fundamentals occur as separate pods of information that will coalesce as you proceed. Part One is a system in itself: The principles are presented in a linear format and they build upon each other. Be sure to work through the chapters in sequence.

Part Two is a collection of essays that enhance and bolster the precepts discussed in Part One. Its structure is more relaxed so, although I recommend you also read Part Two's chapters in sequence, feel free to browse if that's what works for you.

And there's a slightly meditative bearing throughout. But navel gazing exasperates me, so you won't find endless-loop psychobabble. This book would have been shorter if I had decided to deliver these precepts as "Sam's Top Ten Tips for Getting What You Want." (You can thank me now for not doing that to you.) But these pages are indeed a mental exercise that will lead to something profound—an internal getting-it-in-the-guts revelation that will change everything.

My business book, *Work the System: The Simple Mechanics of Making More and Working Less* precedes *Mindset* by eight years. The intended market for each is different (*Work* is for business owners; *Mindset* is for everyone else), but the message is precisely the same.

Work has been revised and updated nine times through three editions, so I've settled on certain words and turns of phrase that best help me explain the methodology. I'll use some of those words and phrases here in *Mindset*, because they have served me well in that book as well as in blog posts, interviews, and live presentations.

So what do people want? It's better control over everyday happenings in order to produce freedom. Specifically, I'd say most of us desire

- lots of personal time,
- prosperity,
- physical health,
- emotional serenity,
- solid relationships, and
- the best for those around us.

I'll be presumptuous and assume you agree.

There are two other key concepts that I'll define for you now rather than expect you to absorb through page-by-page osmosis. Both are right-from-the-start important, and they'll immediately make sense. Here they are:

The first is **Point of Sale (POS)**. The term was coined in the retail industry. It describes the efficiency of getting things done in *this* moment, in *this* here and now. Almost always, it's better to get the various wheels of your life rolling immediately and at maximum efficiency. And once you've set them on their way, whenever possible, it's best to have the majority of them rolling ahead unattended by you. Negotiating your days via POS is a logical way to proceed, but it's more profound than that because of the fact that *now is all there is*. The past is altogether gone and, although we certainly must focus on making the future what we want it to be, it remains conjecture. Operating in the present with an eye to the future is the ultimate acknowledgment of reality.

The second key concept is the formula, $1 \rightarrow 2 \rightarrow 3 \rightarrow 4$ = Result. I've touched on this already. Every result (aspect, condition, or situation) of your life right now was preceded by a linear step-by-step process that executed over a period of time. So it logically follows that your future results will be determined by the systems that are executing in *this* moment. Internalize that fact deep down and then join the select few who spend their days inside the left-hand side of the equation, carefully managing the systems of their lives so those systems consistently produce the future results they want. (And where do most people spend their days? On the right-hand side of the equation, fire-killing, constantly trying to straighten out the random bad results that are the products of their unseen and therefore unmanaged systems.)

A metaphor: From your current first-floor living quarters, I'm going to urge you to descend the newly discovered stairway that leads down into the basement. I want you to go down there to see the machines that have been creating your life results back up there on the first floor. And so I'll ask this question again: *When you finally see your systems relentlessly working away down there—the undirected machinery that has been producing the random results upstairs where you live—will you take control of that machinery?* Will you vigorously direct those machines to produce exactly what you want, or will you just turn your back and quietly trundle back upstairs and continue to let them run unattended down there in the basement, churning up the same old random unsatisfactory results?

Does this make sense so far? If so, soon you will be managing the machinery of your life.

For sure, this book isn't Pollyanna thinking, nor will I urge you to go into a feel-good, happy trance. This is about hard, cold reality. Too many people don't deal with raw life as it is! They're doomed to plod through a fantasy world of how they think the world should be rather than dealing with how it really is. Facing reality head-on—whether or not it conforms to preconceived notions—is mandatory if life's machinery is to be properly directed, adjusted, and maintained to produce desired results.

Travel through these pages with me and go beyond the influences of peer pressure, religious dogma, political incantation, family dictate, and/or any other assumptions you've internalized along the way. In our time together, temporarily set aside the menu. You can pick it up again later if that's what you want to do, but for now, to accomplish this take-control transformation, go a layer deeper with me and rely 100 percent on your own gut-level common sense. Let's go to your core, to explore how things work.

And remember that no one out there is monitoring what you think or believe. This is because they're too busy coping with their own personal challenges. You really do live in your own little world, and that's a good thing! And for that matter, don't take my word for any of this. Instead, just take the precepts I present and see if they fit your own experience. This *is* your life, and you get to decide what to do with it.

So in this moment ask yourself, "What is really going on in my world?" Then, ask that question consistently through our time together, and I promise you'll acquire the Systems Mindset in which you'll grasp the logical simple mechanics that propel your existence. Then, after that, you'll fill your days with constant and never-ending System Improvement. Build your life around System Improvement and get the life results you want: more time, money, freedom, and the best for those around you.

And there's this: Despite popular opinion fueled by an unlimited supply of self-help gurus who declare that you must get your mind straight before you can expect any material gain, know that life doesn't work that way. Your personal peace will arrive *after* you secure control of your mechanical world. You can't meditate into bliss if your boss is haranguing you, the mortgage is late, you're forty pounds overweight, and your lover just walked out. Let's first fix the machines of your world so you're resilient and powerful, able to get what you want in your life, and adept at turning life's earthquakes into road bumps. Once you start getting your life under control—and it won't take long—trust that you'll begin to feel a whole lot better about yourself and this world you inhabit.

And yes, I'm a passionate advocate of individual freedom and personal responsibility. I'll get things done myself, thank you, without pointing fingers, expecting someone else to do me a favor, or by petitioning some governmental agency for help. And this positioning isn't just a matter of personal pride, it's about doing what works: no one is going to take you where you want to go. You're going to have to travel there yourself. When you internalize the Systems Mindset and start to note the large number of people who aren't taking charge of their worlds, so often falling into the "I'm a victim" trap, expect to acquire this same slightly utilitarian stance.

Following is a glossary of words, terms, and concepts. It's best to review these interpretations before proceeding.

99.9 percent of everything works fine: Look around! There is a penchant for efficiency in the world. The systems of the world want to work perfectly, and they do.

Circle of influence: Stephen Covey made this concept popular. It refers to the areas of a life in which the individual can affect.

Closed system: A self-contained processing entity, easily discerned from its surroundings.

Control: To dominate; command. Manage.

Error of omission: A less-than-perfect situation that occurs because someone didn't do something.

Fire-killing: Going backward to expend time and energy to repair a problem that should never have happened in the first place.

General Operating Principles: Optional. The second of the three primary Systems Mindset primary documents; a two- to four-page collection of "guidelines for decision making" that is congruent with the Strategic Objective.

Get it, getting it: The deep-down understanding that the world is a collection of separate systems and not a confused mish-mash of happenings.

Linear: This is how systems execute, in a step-by-step progression over time. Within its context, a system is not chaotic. It's logical, reliable, and easy to understand.

Machine: Sometimes visible, sometimes invisible; it is a system, protocol, or process that executes over time to create a result.

Management: The act of directing, handling, guiding, or controlling.

Menu or script: A belief system based on what seems sensible, feels good, or what peers believe (and overtly or covertly expect others to believe). It could be political, national, religious, family, or work based. It feels comfortable and subtly (or not so subtly) promises safety.

One layer deeper: Below the surface of the happenings of our lives, it's where we go to manage the machinery that is creating the results of our individual existences. Spending time down there is how we create personal freedom, wealth, and health, but for most, its existence is masked by the very cacophony its unmanaged systems produce.

Outside and slightly elevated: The essential (and almost metaphysical) perspective. The view downward encompasses everything, including the observer.

Point of sale: Taking action now. It's the antithesis of procrastination.

Primary system: Composed of subsystems, an encapsulated entity with an ultimate purpose.

Recurring system: An enclosed process that executes over and over again.

Strategic Objective: Optional. The first of three primary Systems Mindset documents. It's a single page that defines goals and intended strategies, describes beliefs, lists strengths, and prescribes action.

System, subsystem (or process, protocol, mechanism, mechanics, machine): A self-contained linear framework of moving parts, visible or invisible, all contributing to the singular purpose of producing a result. Within the Systems Mindset context, we are especially interested in recurring systems. The terms system and subsystem are interchangeable depending on context.

System Improvement: The relentless search-and-repair effort of tooling a process closer and closer to perfection in order to prevent recurring problems, increase production and quality, and save time. It is the opposite of fire-killing.

Systems Mindset: The embedded vision of the world as an orderly collection of processes, not as a chaotic mass of sights, sounds, and events. From this more accurate perspective, one creates and adjusts systems so desired results are produced. It's a system in itself, the master regulatory machine for processing a life's happenings.

Systems Mindset Methodology: The mechanical process of establishing goals and then perfecting and maintaining the systems that will ensure the attainment of those goals.

Tweak, tweaking: The antithesis of neglect. The assertive, dogmatic, boots-on-the-ground work of making incremental subsystem enhancements that will ultimately result in a hyperefficient primary system.

Workingman's (or workingwoman's!) philosophy: A set of beliefs stemming from the hard, cold, sometimes dirty realities of life's job site. The pragmatic, formulaic conviction that a carefully composed blueprint that directs the careful assembly of high-quality components will result in an excellent end-product.

Working procedures: Optional. The third of three primary Systems Mindset controlling documents. These are written instructions that describe how more complex (technical specification, listing, checklist, etc.) systems will operate. They are the end products of the System Improvement process.

OK. Let's begin!

PART ONE

THE
MACHINERY

CHAPTER 1

CONTROL IS WHAT YOU WANT

Being a control freak is to be avoided at all costs; people should lighten up and go with the flow. Isn't this culture's incessant search for control the root of the problem?

I could have titled this chapter "Systems Mindset Fundamental Number One." Some people cripple themselves because of a certain brand of political correctness, and it revolves around the obsessive misinterpretation of the word "control." This is a near tragedy because of the dire effect this posture has on their individual lives and to society as a whole. "Seeking control is a bad thing" is a theoretical banality that is stifling a lot of lives. To so many, it just sounds good to declare that seeking control is a callous thing, that rather, it's oh-so-sensitive to go with the flow, to not strive so hard to be in the driver's seat. And yet a modicum of quiet observation reveals that, for any of us, getting through the day is an epic quest to gain more control than we have.

To make things better for ourselves we constantly assume a third-party personal management stance, doggedly analyzing what we think, say, eat, and how we comport ourselves, how hard we work, how we spend our free time, how we relate to the people around us, how much we are willing to give (and take, and understand), and how we want to be perceived, all while expecting serenity to just happen.

For each of us, this control-seeking is constant and never ending. It started with our first breath, and it won't end until our last.

Am I suggesting that control-seeking is a bad thing? Not at all. Simply consider the alternative: The opposite of being in control is to be out of control, and it's the out-of-control parts of our lives that cause pain. Is being out of control *ever* a good thing?

No one is immune to the control quest. So why do so many condemn it? Doesn't it make better sense to improve the process?

And in this effort to get more personal control, I'm not talking about victimizing others or plundering the environment. It's too bad so many people equate seeking personal control with causing harm.

It's ironic, but a rejection of control-seeking is, in itself, an assertion of control.

–

OK, I'll consider that. So where do I start?

First, find a way to control *you*. So for starters, accept that having more control is a good thing and then thoughtfully seek it, but only within your circle of influence. ("Circle of influence" is a great term, don't you think? It's Stephen Covey's gem.)

To illustrate: Within your circle, you can manage the development of a particular skill and then, in practicing it, the skill will become more honed, more complex, more controlled. How about making more money, finding new friends, or getting fit? It's the same thing as you act within your circle: Get good at what you do. As you improve your expertise in a particular area, pay attention to feedback, tweak incessantly, and become more efficient at creating value for others, and getting ahead will happen almost spontaneously. Becoming adept at anything has everything to do with gaining more control.

The consequence? Getting efficient inside your circle of influence is how the circle gets larger.

–

Isn't the quest for money and domination a huge problem?

That's a general misconception. Money is an inanimate tool. That's it. I used to think the pursuit of money turned people bad, but I was wrong. The selfish/greed element is always out there, but even that is not about money or the lack of it. It's about control, and problems ensue when you either demand too much of it or tolerate having too little. So your best bet is to stay within your circle and take the necessary steps to manage yourself, to get your own self under control. Sometimes it's cleaning the house. Sometimes it's breaking off a relationship or doing what is necessary to begin a new one. Other times it's executing a business deal, and all the time it includes routine inside-the-circle mechanical work: eating right, exercising, finding enough sleep, fulfilling responsibilities, and treating other people with respect.

Think about this over the next couple of days as you go about your regular business: Analyze a particular problem you have, one that is especially bothersome. Does it seem to be rooted in money or relationships or health? Go one layer deeper and see that it's really about control.

As an example, let's talk about control within a family. This is what works: The parent and the child are not pals. The parent is the parent, and the child is the child. The parent acts like a parent and exerts respectful control over the child. The mechanical reality is that the parent must ultimately direct things if family life is to stay orderly and constructive, and the child can develop a spine and learn to respect others.

The posture assumes the child will be a parent one day, too, in control and responsible for preparing yet another child to be an adult.

–

If I look at things in this way, it seems my marriage is a battle for control. What can I do?

Here's a concept that's central to the Systems Mindset vision. Get "outside and slightly elevated" of the particular situation. Together, both of you take a position where you look down on this thing called the marriage relationship. Never mind the individual personalities and consider the relationship as a separate closed system: two people in a pact with certain needs, expectations, and goals. This is the external perspective in which the linear, mechanical dynamics of a system can be analyzed without a power struggle ensuing. Ask, what are the unemotional, mechanical rules of this marriage? Get specific about the details. For instance, when exactly is my time mine, and your time yours? How, precisely, is the money to be spent? Who earns the money? Who manages it? What are our promises to each other—clearly defined promises that have to be kept to preserve trust and the marriage itself?

Eckhart Tolle talks about this "outside" concept in the first pages of his book *The Power of Now*. In his dark days, there came a moment when he said to himself, "I can't live with myself anymore!" In that observation in which he was involuntarily thrust outside of his own self and was able to look down on his existence, he discovered, "There are two of me, the watcher and the watched." How profound, as he realized for the first time that there were two of him, and that through his new outside positioning he could choose which one would be in control! He then acted upon this simple insight by assertively managing himself, and then he built a life of contribution.

So with your partner, see the marriage as the independent mechanism that it is. To negotiate a relationship in this way is refreshing and exciting.

–

How is a health problem related to control?

In any instance of illness or injury there is some degree of anxiety caused by the decrease in normal functionality. A virulent strain of cancer is perhaps the most vivid illustration of this, whereby the ultimate loss of control, death, is a real possibility.

–

What about work? I'm a manager and can't get control of my staff. I can't convince them to do things the way I want them to be done.

Your business department is your responsibility, so it's within your circle. It's your machine, your primary system. (And this primary system is made up of subsystems. And yes, you can consider your staff—and your own self—as subsystems within this primary system that is your department.) You want to be outside-and-slightly-elevated as you see them and yourself functioning down there. Within a business, a vital step in applying the Systems Mindset effectively is to ask staff to list, in black and white, the precise sequential steps of the execution of their various work processes. Then, ask them what they think and how they would go about performing their duties. If their recommendations are sensible, you implement them. Then, turn your people loose, giving them support, the tools they need, and rewards when they achieve what you want them to achieve. Do this, and the cooperation you seek will enter through the side door, with enthusiastic employees willing to give 100 percent, because they are part of the decision-making process and are being properly compensated for their good work.

For now, at this early stage of the book, especially focus on this Systems Mindset premise: *Personal control is a good thing, and you want as much of it as you can get.*

CHAPTER 2

THE FRENETIC LIFE

My life is hectic. Too often I feel confused and just can't seem to get things done. If I back off and take a breath, I feel guilty. If I proceed, I make a mistake. Life is chaotic and I feel trapped. Is it me?

Well, yes, it is you, but that's a good thing, because you can fix you. You are the supreme commander of you!

Up until seventeen years ago my life was a swirling, confused ordeal. Yet in a flash of insight, at a specific moment in time that I vividly recall, the chaos disappeared for good.

Because the new vision enabled me to create the conditions in my life that I wanted, my first effort was to forge all the free time and money I needed, and that's what I did. Immediately upon experiencing the insight, my business and personal life began to improve, and I've been incrementally building value ever since.

This is what I want for you: to experience the Systems Mindset insight and then create exactly the life of freedom and wealth and peace you've always wanted.

But let's start by tackling the elephant in the living room, what may be your largest challenge in acquiring the Systems Mindset. Although this particular elephant isn't the subject of the book, it's the reason most people can't even get started in the process of securing the personal control they need to effectively manage their lives. It's the plague of what I call DDD: Digital Drug Dementia, the mental-paralysis epidemic that is ignored even though, or maybe because, most people are infected. It's the primary reason for personal flakiness. (Flaky people are everywhere. Have you noticed?) DDD is the reason most people can't concentrate, and concentration is mandatory if there is to be action one layer deeper: down in that place where life results are created.

DDD detracts from every facet of a life and makes it impossible to break free, so let's see if it's a problem for you. (If it *is* a problem and you're not willing to deal with it, then no matter what you learn here, getting a grip on things is going to be tough.)

–

OK. I admit it. I'm a bit flaky. How did I get this way? Just how big a problem is it?

I should qualify this. It's OK if you're a little flaky because, for good reason, a tendency in that direction is part of the human condition. Thoughts race through our heads in a sequence that is not always logical, but this rapid thought fluidity, fostered over eons, gives us quick adaptability to the rushing torrent of the world. This wonderful ability to adapt is why we humans are at the top of the food chain. Our experience varies moment to moment, and we adjust quickly to the ever-changing stimulus: first we try this, then we try that, and then we go in yet another direction to see what happens next. We're experts at instantly adjusting to circumstance: listening, talking, thinking, analyzing, testing, seizing opportunity, changing our minds, learning, and taking action *right now* due to the new information that just popped up.

It's the human gift that our brains are fluid and able to move fast, so don't waste mental energy thinking it's an internal dysfunction.

But this incredible agility—our innate capacity to turn on a dime—is also an open door for the DDD elephant to charge into the living room and take up residence, paralyzing our ability to focus.

What is the digital component of the DDD plague? It began sixty years ago as TV made its debut and our culture first met the screen. It's the media we absorb; it's the devices we respond to throughout the day, our attention flitting from one thing to the next. We're moving fast, fast, fast! It's the steady onslaught of email and social media: Texting! Twitter! Facebook! And it's the passive entertainment, too, including TV, movies, and portable music devices with their infernal earbuds that lock us in our cages no matter what else we might be doing.

There's online gaming, too. It goes on and on . . .

Bam! Bam! Bam! We lurch from one topic to another hundreds of times—thousands of times—each day, and a lot of us have become quite good at it. And in all of this we don't get much practice concentrating. Truth is, we learn how *not* to concentrate, becoming experts at shallow-thinking multitasking.

And we get impatient with ourselves and with others, wanting answers now!

Look around at any cluster of people and see how many are mentally extracted from the real-time events of the moment, hammering away on a smartphone or plugged into music.

It's not just that our concentration abilities have been crippled in this focus-hostile world. As we're swallowed up by our devices, we don't think creatively. Why? Because we don't need to. Information is ceaselessly delivered to us, and for a huge swath of humanity it's not necessary to think originally, so it doesn't happen much. Instead, we absorb, with even further attention span diminishment. You know it's true.

The screen delivers gobs of information, and we acquiesce to what feels best *right now*. There's a huge stream of random input, but not a lot of output.

Have you heard the adage that "your strongest point is also your weakest point?" It's a cogent observation, and here it's illustrated perfectly: Our instant adaptability delivers flightiness as a by-product.

Here's a quote from the preface of my book, *Work the System*:

> In the past thirty years the lure of instant gratification has seized a huge chunk of our population. For members of the hooked-up generation, too many with the attention span of a gnat—addicted to smartphones, preoccupied with social media, and dumbed-down by the silliness of much of the media and entertainment industries—it's a stretch to slow down to consider the root of things. The nervous gratification of the moment is a distraction from the quiet contemplation of the reasons why events unfold as they do. Today, unlike twenty years ago, a good now is available by just plugging in and tuning out. For too many of us, slowing down to examine things is not entertaining, and that's too bad because it's mandatory that we take the time to understand the machinery of our lives if we are to modify that machinery to produce the results we desire.

That's bad enough. Now, add the drug component of DDD. Especially in the US, back in the sixties, mind-altering substances made their wholesale introduction and are now, fifty years later, socially acceptable. Yes, there has always been alcohol, nicotine, and caffeine, but they were ingested sporadically with the understanding they were probably not all that good for us. Twenty-five years ago, the social acceptance of prescribed mood adjusters began. (In those days it began with Prozac for adults and Ritalin for children.) Now, the legalization of marijuana is front and center.

People don't just think it's OK, they think it's necessary.

In the West, consider that 80 percent of us drink caffeine to the point of addiction, while here in the United States, any number of surveys show that 10 to 12 percent of the adult population uses antidepressants, with each individual convinced that their brain cells are somehow not active enough.

And what about alcohol? Ten percent of us are alcoholics. Add in nicotine and all the other legal and illegal substances, and it's safe to say that 98 percent of us ingest some form of mood-adjusting substance every day.

(Regarding the social acceptance of it all, here's something that popped up this early September morning as I am working on the last run-through of this manuscript and, in fact, while I was reviewing this very chapter. At first I saw it as a synchronicity or a coincidence, but now I'm quite sure it's neither. It's just how things are out there now. Here's what happened: As I took a breather from concentrating on these words, here in my office at Centratel, I wandered back to the break room where the local newspaper had just appeared on the lunch table. What was the above-the-fold headline that caught my eye? Here it is: "Park District Evolves on Alcohol: It Plans to Start Selling." Read that again and notice the word "evolves" was used, suggesting the Parks Department, in this decision, has reached a higher plane of consciousness.)

But my point is not about the good or bad of it—there's no moral judgment here—it's about the naked fact that if foreign substances are ingested into the body system, thinking becomes impaired, and impaired thinking is the antithesis of mental acuity.

Our preoccupation with drug and alcohol ingestion, combined with the pervasiveness of our electronic gizmos, gives us the freneticism of DDD. It's everywhere: at work, at home, in our schools . . . , and it's worse now than it was just a few years ago.

And so, for most of us, our attention spans have been abbreviated and we're hyper as we flit from here to there at the mercy of external and internal stimuli. We can't focus! It's our kids who especially suffer, having no clue that they're stumbling, because they've never experienced a relaxed, uninterrupted day. They don't know about calm. They haven't learned to sit still, uninterrupted, and quietly think things through. (I recently asked Lexi, my fourteen-year-old granddaughter, "Do you and your friends *really* text each other hundreds of times a day?" Her quiet and unapologetic answer was, "Yeah.")

So, we have an enormous capacity to adapt to a changing environment, and that's exactly what we've done. Though our brains were not designed for inane distraction and chemical assaults, they are stimulus-response miracles and have dutifully adapted. *We're multitasking marvels, but part of the price we pay is a brain that only functions in short bursts, and that unfocused mental comportment simply isn't effective for achieving long-term goals, and worse, it stunts the possibility of being enthralled with the everyday life that surrounds us.*

The other part of the price to be paid is the wasted time and effort expended on the inanity. What if that same time and energy were expended on creating something of long-term value, for instance, something that could lead to personal freedom?

The most obvious indicator of DDD is the inability to sit down and read a book. These days, outside of academia, it doesn't happen much. The reason that reading a book is a lost art is because most people can't get through a single paragraph without being interrupted by their own wired minds, thus making the effort frustrating and unrewarding. It's too hard to focus.

Because it's the easy way out for our minds, we're more comfortable being swallowed up and engulfed rather than sitting still to contemplate.

In his breakthrough book, *The Shallows*, Nicholas Carr says, "The computer screen bulldozes our doubts with its bounties and convenience. It is so much our servant that it would seem churlish to notice that it is also our master." Carr continues, "Over the last years I've had the uncomfortable sense that someone, or something, has been tinkering with my brain, remapping the neural circuitry, reprogramming the memory."

Indeed, our minds have adapted!

But Carr delivers this ironic good news: Reading a book is the antidote. Because our brains are incredibly adaptable, and even after years of electronically shortened attention spans and too much stimulant of one kind or another, they can relearn to focus in a matter of days. Carr specifically recommends a book, not a magazine or a newspaper, each of which has a flighty here-and-then-there quality. What about using a Kindle or other e-reader? For attention-span therapy, they are not as effective as the hard copy.

And Carr says there is no reason to go Luddite by giving up our electronic pals. We'll learn more about communication strategies in chapter 28.

Yes, pick up that book as you reject those state-of-mind altering substances. Here are actions you can take for quickly regaining focus and getting calm enough—and strong enough—to get your life under better control. Why not start these efforts today, even as you work your way through these pages? Consider these steps as part of an overall preventive primary system that you apply all day long:

- Daily, read a book for at least 30 minutes in a single stretch.
- Stop, or at least cut way back, on mood-adjustment chemicals.

- Limit the TV.
- Reduce the smartphone and social media involvement.

In spare moments that pop up, resist the temptation to check for correspondence (email, texting, etc.) or to report your movements (Facebook, Twitter, etc.). Instead, read the book you've carried along, close your eyes for a brief meditation, or calmly observe what's happening around you.

And so, there's this question: Have we entered the age of narcissism? Yes, probably, but don't concern yourself with societal changes you can't affect. Instead, look to your own life—inside your circle—where you can cause rapid and substantial system improvement.

Enough about the elephant. Let's get to managing the machines of your life.

CHAPTER 3

YOUR LIFE IS A COLLECTION OF SEPARATE SYSTEMS

What?

The Systems Mindset positioning is built around an elementary fact that maybe one in a hundred people detect. Although there are those who were born with the Mindset, most weren't. If it's not innate, acquiring it usually requires three factors.

First, the time must be right, and that usually (but not always) means there has been some recent emotional trauma or there has been a long, drawn-out life hardship that has become unbearable.

Second, the principles must be clearly spelled out.

And third, there must be some quiet, careful observation that is outside of any menu-driven belief system. This doesn't mean the belief system has to disappear; it means that for a short while it is set aside so there can be an unbiased examination of root physical reality.

For many who read these pages, the acquired Systems Mindset insight will come quickly. For others, it will take days or weeks of thinking and observing. It just depends. In any case, for most people the insight appears in a flash, at a specific point in time.

However it arrives, when it happens to you it will be a stark turning point in your life.

Getting the Systems Mindset is a revelation, an enlightenment that will change you forever.

Here is the simple foundational premise of the Systems Mindset: Your life is not a chaotic swirling mass of sights, sounds, and events within which you must incessantly fight for survival. Rather, it's an orderly collection of independent processes, many of which you can quietly adjust so they will deliver you the life experiences you want.

Now it's time for some careful observation.

Look around: in your home, on the street, or at work. Let's start by considering your car, a primary system, which, like any system, is intended to accomplish a task. In this case, the task is to deliver you from point A to point B. And like any primary system, your car is a collection of independent subsystems. Prove that to yourself by asking, what does the radio have to do with the brakes? Or in what way does the transmission affect the air conditioner? And what is the involvement of the headlights with the speedometer?

In each pairing, there is no relationship.

And what about the primary system that is your body? What does your liver have to do with your stomach or your pancreas with your brain? Or, what does your left foot have to do with your right hand? Again, in each matching, nothing!

Yes, in your car and in your body the subsystems are connected to each other and work together to the benefit of the primary system, but in their essence, the subsystems are independent entities.

Your life is a collection of individual systems!

Do you want more evidence? Quietly observe your everyday world. At home you cook a meal. How is that process associated with washing clothes or watching TV or sleeping? And at work, what is the connection between making a sales presentation and preparing the payroll?

Back to your car: The auto mechanic isolates a problem to a particular subsystem and then corrects that problem in that malfunctioning subsystem. Presuming you're dealing with an honest mechanic, if your alternator has failed, that mechanic will not be replacing the fuel pump.

And with your body, if you have a broken leg you won't be rushed to a dermatologist. You're going to be seeing an orthopedic specialist.

This separate-system reality is ubiquitous. Your whole existence and all the world around you is an immense collection of independent systems and subsystems. If you can internalize this fundamental principle, you'll have enormous advantage over those around you. Acquiring this deep understanding is what I call "getting it," and after it happens your future actions will be super efficient, directed by this more accurate comprehension of mechanical reality.

Now let's pause to review what we've learned. In these real-life illustrations, we'll combine two Systems Mindset concepts: the incessant search for control with the reality that life is a collection of independent systems.

Your smartphone: You have it because you need to control your communication.

Your car: You want to determine your physical location so you can control where you are and where you're going.

Your lawnmower: You want control over the grass in your yard.

Your job: You require money, which allows you to exert control in a multitude of areas, so you seek it.

Your house: You want a safe and private location where your body can retreat to rest and recharge.

Your family: You do what you have to do to keep them safe.

Your health: To ensure your continued existence, you do what is necessary to be vital, strong, and injury free.

You can easily come up with more examples, and here's the takeaway: *Via a host of separate processes, our lives are spent in a constant quest for control.*

Have you ever thought of your life in this way?

—

But still, if I focus on gaining more control, won't I become a control freak?

Yes, but not in the colloquial sense. In your new control-seeking efforts you're going to quietly get what you want in your life without driving yourself and everyone around you crazy. You'll be passionate about your new vision, but your management efforts will certainly not be due to some kind of obsessive-compulsive malady.

There it is: the simple mechanics of the life you live and the world you inhabit. Now you're one layer deeper than almost everyone around you. This elementary adjustment in how you see the components of your world will guide you to make decisions that will take you straight to the freedom and personal control you've always wanted.

Again, I call this perspective the Systems Mindset.

CHAPTER 4

THE UNIVERSAL FORMULA FOR HOW THINGS HAPPEN

Let's go backward a bit: How exactly do you define a system?

A system is a linear sequence of steps that execute over time, leading to a result. In your kitchen, your toaster is a system. After a couple of minutes of operation, the toaster's result is a slightly charred slice of bread. From the TV system, you're delivered information and entertainment over various periods of time. The system of the hand at the end of your wrist gives you a multitude of results all having to do with the physical manipulation of external objects—each instance of which takes some amount of time to accomplish.

And your relationships and informal communication protocols are systems, too, creating, over time, results. You can't touch these systems, though, because there is no physicality.

Here is an interesting nuance, and it's a bit on the subjective side, but as the years have passed I've become more certain of it: Systems *want* to execute properly to produce their intended results. There is some intangible power that drives them forward. Even very basic systems have an internal spirit that moves them toward completion. The true proof of this is in nature. What makes the grass grow and the seasons change? There is something enthralling out there, propelling things forward. Call it God or the Universal Life Force or whatever you want, there is a power surrounding us that very much wants systems to execute to completion.

—

You talk of a simple perspective change that will make everything better. Is that really possible?

Your new stance will enable you to solve the vast majority of your problems because you will be delving into the actual system mechanics of your life. You'll be traveling to the place where your life-result systems are operating so you can tweak those systems to produce the exact results you want.

Here it is: *To get desired outcomes, you must direct the machinery that produces the outcomes.* Again: Most people don't see the systems of their lives so they don't manage them, and unmanaged systems produce random results.

You don't want random results! It's a numbers game, and indiscriminate results will not often be congruent with your goals. You want the exact outcomes you desire.

This is foundational to the Systems Mindset, and I summarized it in the Introduction: *In this moment, every condition of your life was preceded by a linear process that executed over time.* Consider the following, what I call the Universal Formula for How Things Happen: $1 \rightarrow 2 \rightarrow 3 \rightarrow 4$ = Result. This squarely explains how reality unfolds on planet earth: *Things happen in sequence over time.* One leads to two, two leads to three, three leads to four, etc. Once a process has completely executed—it might have been four steps or it might have been four hundred—the result appears. This is cold, hard, unemotional physical reality.

This was in the introduction too: *The systems of your life are executing all the time. You can't turn them off. The conditions of your existence are the products of these relentlessly executing individual machines—machines that will remain invisible and unmanaged—or, through the Systems Mindset, machines that you will choose to see and then direct.*

Think about your immediate surroundings right now. At this precise point in time as you contemplate these words, where are you? Are you at work or at home? Are you on vacation somewhere? Do you find yourself in a subway or on an airplane, or in bed preparing to go to sleep? Now, I ask, where were you physically before you arrived at this place that you occupy now? What were the steps you took to travel from that previous place to where you are in this very moment? Did you walk? Did you drive? Did you ride a bicycle or take public transportation? Did you step onto a train or into a plane? Did you walk from your living room into your bedroom? If you're listening to these words in audio, did you step into your car before you started listening? Or, if you're jogging and listening, where were you physically located ten minutes ago? Three minutes ago? One minute ago?

However you arrived at this place that you occupy now, know this for sure: There were steps that executed one after the other, over time, that delivered you here.

In this illustration, the getting-there process—the part that executed over time—is the $1 \rightarrow 2 \rightarrow 3 \rightarrow 4$ component of the Universal Formula. Where you are right now, exactly in this moment, is the Result.

Let's go through some other scenarios. Assume you're married. How did you get to the actual marriage? Were there years of courtship? Or months? Did you fall in love? (In many cultures, marriage is arranged.) How is the marriage right now? Your relationship as it is in this very moment, represented by the Results side of the equation, is the end product of the 1→2→3→4 part of the equation, the part that occurred over time.

How about your high school education that led up to your diploma? What was the process necessary to get the diploma? Did you go through four years of public or private high school? Or, over some duration of time, were you home-schooled?

What about your refrigerator? How did it come to be where it is? (Chances are you or someone else visited an appliance outlet or shopped online, considered various models, made the purchase, and arranged the delivery.)

Look at the details and conditions of your life in this moment (e.g., the shoes on your feet, your car, your friends, your family, your job, your body). Can you, considering them one at a time, visualize the systematic steps over time that delivered them to you—exactly as they are—in this here and now?

The Universal Formula fits everything. Here it is again: 1→2→3→4 = Result. There is no disputing that each result of your life came about because of a series of steps that executed over a period of time. This is how things happen!

–

So how does this affect me?

What if, one by one, you isolated the various critical systems of your life and then spent significant time improving the efficiency of each? And, at the same time, what if you isolated the systems in your life that are holding you back and then consciously removed them?

If you made these improvements, do you think your life would get better?

This is the absurdly simple blueprint: *If you put consistent effort into system improvement; you'll reach your goal of living the exact life you want.*

There is nothing mysterious here, nothing esoteric. There's no cluttered and abstract theory. It's just simple, real-world mechanics.

And so *it makes sense for you to immerse yourself in performing system improvements, to spend a lot of time doing it.* And what is the additional bonus beyond living the exact life you want? Because the systems approach is about how the machinery of life really works, you will become enchanted with simple reality. Life will become stunning just as it is.

Here's what I want to hammer home: *Since it's incontestable that every future result in your life will be preceded by a linear process that executes over time, you must spend focused, deliberate effort—in this moment—managing those processes.*

Oh, and what of those systems you can't adjust, because they are not in your control? Relax. If you can't fix something, forget it. Metaphorically speaking, if you don't like the TV program, change the channel or turn off the set.

And know that as you manage these machines of your life—as you adjust them so they become more efficient and more powerful, producing better and better results—your circle will expand. How much time should you spend managing the systems of your life? I'd say, a lot. The more time you spend in this System Improvement place, the more you will get what you want in your life.

Again: Seen or not seen, managed or not managed, the visible and invisible processes of your world execute. They're working hard all the time, churning away in this very moment as you read these words.

Know this for sure: Too many people spend their time in the Results part of the 1→2→3→4 = Result formula, frittering away time and energy trying to repair the random bad consequences of their unseen and therefore unmanaged systems.

So, yet again, here's the vital question: If you can see that the machines of your life have been executing randomly, are you going to get in there and get them straightened out?

–

But doesn't everything happen for a reason?

As it is usually applied, this is an annoying platitude not grounded in reality. It sounds good. It's why we hear it all the time, but think about it. The inference is that God is watching over us and knows better than we do about what should happen next. If something goes wrong, well, that's OK, because God made that happen and we should just conjure up a smile and go with the flow. I viscerally disagree. *Yes, every "thing" does happen for a reason, but the reason for each of those things is the linear system that preceded and then produced it.*

Is God involved? I'm certain of it. But God's gift to us is not a preordained future or a series of divine blessings we've earned through prayer, good deeds, or deep faith. God's gift is bigger than that. It's that every one of us has been granted the power to choose and act, to adjust the mechanical elements of our lives to make things better. The question is, do we put that power to good use?

I thank God for giving me the ability to see one layer deeper, for the capacity to adjust the things of my world in order to make them what I want them to be.

My special blessing, and yours, is the Systems Mindset.

CHAPTER 5

GO ONE LAYER DEEPER

This is the "crux" chapter. It's written in a more meditative tone, and there's some review. If it hasn't struck you already, here's the point where you might acquire the Systems Mindset. Read slowly, carefully contemplating your life.

–

You want me to go "one layer deeper"? Help me go there.

Let's use what we've learned and tackle this with an analogy. Imagine a small house. You've lived in this house for a long, long time. It's single story, and inside is everything in your life, including the TV, coffee maker, dog, furniture, your clothes, and even your significant other and your job. In the house is everything you are, too. Your college degree (or lack thereof) is also there, as are your relationships with your lover, relatives, friends, and colleagues. Your health and personality take up residence, too. How you look, how you communicate with others, your politics, even your personal habits are all there. Everything about you occupies this little house.

This dwelling represents surface reality, your total accumulation of life results: the elements, conditions, relationships, and situations of your existence. And if you're like most people, you are ceaselessly shuffling these life parts around, attempting to get them to form a pattern that will deliver life control: freedom, peace, the best for those around you, and the ability to have the future turn out the way you want it to turn out.

And if you feel that sometimes you're beating yourself to death to live the existence you want, here's what's up: *Your world is unsatisfactory because you are not deliberately and intensely controlling the machinery that creates your life results.* The results you are getting are random, and that means they are not often the results you want. This accumulation of assorted consequences delivers an existence that is chaotic and unsatisfying.

So back to the house analogy. Imagine that this house has a secret, hidden basement. You didn't know it was down there until this moment. It's filled with the machines—the systems, the processes—that produce the results of your life, upstairs where you live. Via the $1\rightarrow2\rightarrow3\rightarrow4$ = Result formula, this machinery is working 24/7/365 to produce the elements of your world upstairs, good and bad.

Whether you see this machinery or not, it's grinding away every minute to produce your life components. And it will continue to grind away tomorrow and next week and next year. It will never let up until your dying moment.

Because the machinery has been invisible, you haven't directed it, adjusted it, or maintained it. How could you?

But now, today, in this moment, on these pages, you're here with me in this house, and I've just shown you the hidden doorway that leads to a stairway that goes down into the basement, the basement full of machinery you didn't know was there.

Now you're tentatively descending the stairs as I stay up on the first floor, standing in the open door, watching, encouraging you to continue downward. Halfway down the staircase you see, for the first time, the scores of machines nestled side-by-side, quietly rumbling away as they work. These are the system machines that have been generating the random outcomes of your life upstairs on the first floor. You stand there on the stairway, watching the machinery churn.

You just "got" how your life operates!

And now that you see the machinery, your next move is obvious, isn't it? Of course it is. You will quickly—right now!—finish descending the stairs into the basement and immediately start to adjust those machines, one at a time, so each produces precisely the results you desire upstairs.

All of a sudden, you're a mechanic.

And what of the future? You will spend much time in the basement. You'll *want* to spend time down there, making adjustments, creating new machines and removing others, because every time you finish working down there and ascend those stairs back up to the first floor, you'll see that your results have improved. Up there, life is fuller and richer and more satisfying. Things just seem to click along better and better.

Your life is improving because of the work you've been performing down there in the basement. You'll be getting what you want, and your self-confidence will surge.

So to achieve success, stop trying to rearrange the bad results of unseen and therefore unmanaged systems. That's fire-killing. Instead, see and then manage your machinery so it produces the results you desire.

There's nothing airy-fairy here. It's all mechanical. And this is why the Systems Mindset is more than theory and even more than pure mechanics: It's nothing less than spiritual. It's an outright acknowledgment of the miracle of the everyday sights, sounds, and events of your life! The machinery was always there, working away. You just didn't see it until now.

–

Is this failure to see the machinery what causes fire-killing?

Indeed! For most people, the machinery in the basement is invisible as it ceaselessly churns out random outcomes upstairs, random outcomes that must be adjusted. Life becomes absorbed with fire-killing.

What a tedious way to live!

But never mind that. Today you're going to stop being a fire-killer and become a fire-prevention specialist.

Your next moves will be to use your surface-reality observations to guide you to do what must be done down below. While you're getting through the day upstairs, you'll always remember there is a basement full of systems machinery and that you must, whenever you can, go down there to make sure those machines are working properly.

–

Sounds great. But I doubt it's this simple. What you're describing sounds like an "easy button."

Well, it *is* an easy button. The moment you acquire the Systems Mindset, your faith in how the machinery of your life operates will be as strong as your certainty that gravity holds you to the earth. There will be no doubt because the proof will be in your new successes.

Once you see the machinery, getting what you want in your life will be a simple thing.

–

Will you tell me more about this "get it" experience?

For one thing, once you achieve the Systems Mindset, you will never go back to your previous way of thinking. You can't go back! And again, about the awakening itself: It almost always comes in a flash, in a specific and unexpected moment. Maybe you'll be at work, or it will be the very first thought on your mind when you wake up one morning, or you'll be in a crowded airport, or perhaps in these moments while you're reading these pages, or weeks from now after you've finished this book, lounging around doing nothing at all. You never know when it will happen, but it's mind-bending when it does, and it's a moment you won't forget. Seventeen years ago it struck me, and I can remember every nuance of the event as it permanently changed my life in that instant. I can describe that experience in a single word: delicious.

When it happens to you, you'll never be the same.

CHAPTER 6

99.9 PERCENT OF EVERYTHING WORKS JUST FINE

OK, OK! This all seems great for my own situation, but there is so much wrong in the world! What about that?

Your premise is inaccurate. Of course there are situations out there that are seriously bothersome, but it's an error to conclude that the world is overall problematic.

Right now, no matter where you are, look around. Can't you see the perfection? If you're inside your house or apartment, what do you observe? In the kitchen, is the water coming out of the tap when you turn the knob? Is the heating or air-conditioning working? Is your TV turning on? What about the electricity? How about your smartphone? And your heart? Is it beating? What about your brain? Is it thinking? Is there oxygen in the air? Are you breathing?

Yes, I know. On a personal level, sometimes the car doesn't start, and once in a while the electricity fails. And I don't make light of the fact that people get sick and some have physical disabilities. Still, in the numbers game, which is a hard and cold evaluation of the whole package, my 99.9 percent statistic holds up.

Regarding global affairs: Yes, of course, we humans have a penchant for horribly gumming up the works (ask a Christian in Libya or an inner-city teen). Psychological, political, relational, and personal health dysfunction are evident, yet the vast majority of people in the world are fed and warm and safe.

The idea that the things of the world are good is a revelation to nearly everyone. Why? Much of it has to do with the media which does everything possible to seize our attention. Simply put: Good news doesn't sell, so we're delivered the morbid, which is invariably more interesting. Most of us equate what we see and read and watch with typical reality. *Truth is, what is presented to us in the media is a rooted-out tiny slice of what isn't OK, and it's a profound miscalculation to generalize about the world's condition from that anecdotal evidence, anecdotal evidence propagated by people with an agenda.* Unless you live in a part of the world that is a hotbed of dysfunction, your life is probably pretty good.

The other reason we tend to see the world as overall problematic is that when personal bad news crops up, it demands our full attention. But don't you agree that an immediate problem that sours everything in the moment doesn't indicate the whole world is a mess?

And this point is critical: *If you find yourself in a bad state of mind or outright depressed, that doesn't mean life isn't good. It just means your immediate mental comportment isn't good.* Think of the people you've seen who are physically attractive and healthy and who have lots of money, power, fame, and a future full of possibilities, but are miserable. Their worlds are, in the mechanical sense, near perfect, but their states of mind stink! Do not equate your immediate negative emotional state with the condition of the world.

–

This is not something I hear every day. What else can you tell me?

Let's review this: Because the elements of a system execute according to their own construction to produce a result, you have incredible power if you stay within your circle to work on your own systems, the systems you can actually affect. This is where you can make things better. Don't beat your head against the wall trying to adjust things outside your circle. (As an aside, it's my guess that the term "raving lunatic" came about in order to describe people who spend all their time outside their circles, trying to rally support to fix things that can't be fixed.)

Here's something further: If you personally don't like a system's result, strictly speaking that's not because of an error in the system. That system is working perfectly according to its construction. If you want a different result from a system, you must go inside it and adjust its configuration. Once you've made that adjustment, the system will continue to operate perfectly—according to its new construction—only now it will be producing the result you want.

The wonderful spiritual by-product of the Systems Mindset is that when you see the perfection of the universe, the flawed visions that the media and entertainment cabals thrust upon you—and the immediate problems you may encounter—are much less onerous. When the Systems Mindset struck me so many years ago, I was dumbfounded to realize that my life had been dictated by my certainty that the world was a hostile place, that I was always on the brink of destruction. I had lived my whole life like that! But now I see the world as it truly is: a beautifully synchronized collection of independent systems, every one of which is operating exactly as constructed.

(But here's the qualification that I touched upon earlier: In this world that is an immense collection of systems, man-caused interference is huge. How can anyone deny pollution and wars as we disrupt perfect natural systems, as well as human systems that were previously working just fine? There's no question that the human negative aspects of fear, ego, greed, etc. are the root cause of the interferences. But still, those interferences don't negate the fact that the systems of the world are dependable, propelled by an invisible force that not only pushes them toward completion of their individual missions, but also relentlessly works to repair any damage. In any case, despite human interference and the resulting damage—and here's where pragmatism enters—the huge majority of lives are surrounded by perfection.)

And so for you, since 99.9 percent of everything works fine, there probably isn't that much for you to adjust in order to obtain the exact results you want. We'll talk more of this in the next chapter.

–

If this is all true, we're talking about a stunningly positive change in my life.

No kidding! The realization that your personal world is in great shape is, to understate it, an exciting revelation. It will be electrifying when you grasp the truth of it and start to observe your life more accurately, when you begin to get your machinery pointed in the right direction and operating efficiently.

–

Now I see this could almost be a spiritual thing. Is there anything I can do to make the internal awakening come sooner?

Yes, and you don't need a guru, peer group approval, or blind faith. You just need you. *The spiritual is right here, right now, if you choose to see it!* Just keep your eyes open and observe the events of your day from your new outside and slightly elevated perch. Your epiphany will arrive when you least expect it.

–

But what about the past? How about my future?

The past is gone, but value it in a peripheral way for two obvious reasons. First, some of it might emerge in some way to affect your current decisions. So be prepared for that. And second, you've learned some things along the way that will prove useful down the line.

But don't regret the past or wallow in it. It simply doesn't exist, and for that matter neither does the future (although you certainly want to prepare for it).

There is only this moment in time.

One day soon you'll acquire the Systems Mindset, and you will feel the truth of it in your belly. Then you'll immediately begin to act on your new vision, applying it moment to moment, not just because it makes sense and not just because you will see huge improvements in your life, but especially because life, as it is, has become amazing.

–

I'll still have personal problems though, right?

Of course, for anyone, no matter their state of mind, problems will arrive, one by one, in sequence and sometimes more than one at a time. But in living via the Systems Mindset you'll find you're dealing with far fewer, and those particular problems won't be as overwhelming as they would have been. You'll be resilient and powerful, in control.

And here's something else about your Systems Mindset: When there is a problem within your circle of influence, you'll be thankful because it will be a red flag alerting you to make a System Improvement so that particular problem won't ever happen again. You'll learn that glitches are your friends because they point out where improvements can be made. And every time a System Improvement is made, that system gets more efficient and reliable. (It's a beautiful thing! Imagine systems getting better and better over time, rather than wearing out!)

–

But one system can interfere with another system, right?

Yes, indeed! And this is a primary concern: System A gumming up the works of system B. Not limited to greed or incompetence, there are many reasons this can happen, and we must work to insulate our systems from this kind of interference.

The perfect examples of one nefarious system interfering with another perfectly good system? Organized crime and government intrusion into our personal affairs. (Oh, but I repeat myself . . .)

CHAPTER 7

THERE'S NOT THAT MUCH TO FIX

So, this is a numbers game?

This Systems Mindset fundamental deserves its own chapter.

Briefly, let's cover this important point again: My proposition that the world is operating almost flawlessly is in the statistics, that by tallying the numbers you can see that we live in a remarkable world. Yes, as we discussed, there are situations that we wish were different, but here's the thing: No matter the problems, 99.9 percent of the subsystems of the world, including your world, are executing perfectly. And so, that means that if your life is problematic, there isn't that much repair work to perform.

Once you can see the separate systems of your life, three things happen. First, you realize that you have more power than you previously thought you had. Second, you begin to work within your circle. And third, you find yourself eagerly discarding those few dysfunctional primary systems that have been dragging you down.

–

Is there more to repair in a business, or in personal life?

At the risk of braggadocio, I'll tout my answering service business, Centratel, which I've owned and operated for more than thirty years. It's an entity with thousands of wheels spinning simultaneously, 24/7, and because my staff and I incessantly focus on perfecting the machines of it, little goes wrong. *We relentlessly tend to the machines that produce the results. It's what we do all day long.* And when a problem occasionally arises, we don't just repair the immediate damage. More importantly, we go into the relevant system to make an adjustment so the problem never occurs again. This is why we don't have many problems!

Dysfunction at Centratel? Not so much.

But that's a business. Private life can be simpler than business life, but problems can sometimes be more difficult to repair—family relationships in particular. Within a business there are formal and informal codes of communication and responsibility, and there's a chain of command in which an ongoing problem in a relationship can be solved by the departure of one of the individuals in the relationship. Removal of one party or the other is not so easy in a family! So, my condolences if you are faced with a family member who refuses to take a businesslike, systematic, "outside and slightly above" approach to solving a bad situation, and who is not going to be leaving. At least, know that you're not alone: There's a lot of family dysfunction out there.

–

So if I started to repair things now, how much time and work would that entail?

Your beginning efforts will require a bit of extra attention. In fact, for our business coaching and consulting clients we call these first days and weeks (and sometimes, months) the "heavy lifting" phase of the transformation. It really is heavy lifting for a business because of the documentation that must be produced. But for you, the extra time required will be minimal because there will be little documentation. If you choose, simply a personal Strategic Objective and a set of General Operating Principles, and perhaps a few Working Procedures. (I'll talk more about this documentation in chapter 26.)

In the beginning, the extra work is mostly about watching your life from the systems perspective and monitoring yourself so you're keeping your head in the right place. Having said that, it's probable that many of your systems have been neglected to some degree or another, so you will have to examine them and make tweaks where necessary. Also, there will be systems you want to create from scratch, which takes some thought. And, additional head-work will be required in deleting some systems, because the deletions can affect the operation of other systems you are going to keep.

But after a short time the mental workload will drop as you embed the Method, and without any second-guessing, continually tweak your systems.

The bonus is, of course, that the amount of fire-killing in your life will continuously decline until it almost never occurs. Here's what happens: *Your net amount of time spent killing fires will decrease, while your net free time will increase, and one way or another, this incredible efficiency will positively impact your personal financial bottom line.* And this wonderful snowballing scenario doesn't end at some point. It continues on and on: As time goes by, everything gets better.

In discovering the perfection of the systems of your world, you may ask, "How could this be?" and "Who made this happen?" You'll answer that question for yourself, of course. As for me, there's no question that there's something mysterious and powerful behind all these wonderful mechanics. The word "God" works for me.

–

I'm not convinced this isn't just feel-good theory. Where exactly should I start? How can I begin to actually apply the Systems Mindset?

I get that. We've been discussing the mechanical viewpoint, getting outside and slightly elevated, that "repair is minimal," and so on, and I see the question for you is, what exactly do I recommend you do with this information? You want an example of how you can use this in your actual life, right? Before I tell you a great way to put the Systems Mindset to work for the first time, I'll remind you that the positioning will have a positive effect on every aspect of your life. Trust that *when the Systems Mindset epiphany happens, you will look at every decision, large and small, from a different perspective.* For this reason, I won't attempt to list all the things you can do differently. Instead, I'm just going to give you a practical, real-world exercise that will make everything about the Systems Mindset Method crystal clear. It's a "practical workshop for the acquisition of the Systems Mindset." If you have not experienced the epiphany yet, this is a perfect fake-it-until-you-make-it project. The added bonus of this exercise is that, even before it's finished, your personal life will have become considerably more organized and efficient. And note that a number of the principles that I will present in later chapters will reveal themselves to you within this project.

Are you ready to begin?

First, here's a qualifier: You will perform the following exercise in the dwelling where you live: your house, apartment, condo, etc., and in order to keep the instructions simple, I'll refer to where you live, whatever it is, as a "house."

And second, until this exercise is completed, commit to spending a minimum of one hour per day working on it (OK, if it becomes an extensive project, take the weekends off . . .)

Third, you can start this project now or you can start it later, even after you've finished this book. Either way is OK. (Why is it all right to wait? Because, for now, I want to convince you that the Systems Mindset is not theoretical, that it's of practical use, that you can apply it to your day-to-day life right this moment if you choose to do so. But, if you do decide to wait until later, be sure to read through these instructions to the end of the chapter before moving on to chapter 8.)

Fourth, get a pad of paper and a pen ready.

OK, let's start. You are in your house. Stand or sit in your central living area, take a deep breath, slow down, and look around. What do you see? Is it cluttered? Do you know where everything is at a moment's notice? Do you have too much "stuff?" Are there repairs you've been meaning to do but have been putting off? Are there routine upkeep tasks that should have been done by now? Is there something you want to add, an item or a whole system of one kind or another? Are there systems or items to be removed?

For this project—and to begin to practice applying the Systems Mindset—we've just, temporarily, reframed your perception of your house.

Now to further reframe: Mentally divide your house into the separate systems that compose it: the TV, heating and AC system, electrical system, water system, alarm system, walls, floor, ceiling, roof, microwave, blender, coffee maker, lights and lamps, bathroom(s), books, and other static items.

Consider each of these separate systems and ask yourself, which ones are not perfect? Which ones can be improved, repaired, or should be discarded? Use your pen and paper to carefully, stream of thought, make a list.

Now select the system that you most want to modify or fix (or eliminate), and identify it as number one on your list. Then, in order of importance, list numbers two, three, four, etc. You've just created, in order of importance, a list of the separate system improvements you are going to make, the separate system improvements you will execute in order to make your house perfect.

Go to work on the number one system on your list and do what you need to do to enhance it, fix it, or discard it. Complete that system improvement mini-project, then move on to the next most problematic system on your list and do the same. Finish that mini-project.

Then work on the next system improvement, and the next, and the next, until you are finished and your house is perfect.

Investing one hour per day, it may take days or weeks or even months to complete this project. Do you see that in executing this quest you will have assumed an "outside and slightly elevated" positioning from your world in order to consider the separate systems that are within it?

If you complete this exercise in the way I describe here, it's certain that somewhere along the way you will acquire the Systems Mindset.

(And in the process of acquiring it, you will have produced something of significance: a clean, efficient, and beautiful house!)

Now go about doing this same exercise at work, in your relationships, and with your health. That's it! You're now living the Systems Mindset! Your energy is being channeled to System Improvement all day long.

Do you think that once you get a grip on this incredibly potent way of living your life, you'll slip backward?

I'd say, "Not a chance."

In chapter 23 you will encounter some other practical applications of the Mindset, but for now, what I want you to "get" is that the Systems Mindset isn't just theory. It's a real-life, potent life approach that you will use all day long.

So whether you've begun the above "workshop" or not, let's move on to chapter 8.

CHAPTER 8

EMOTIONS FOLLOW MECHANICS

You talk a lot about mechanics, but I believe fixing my life will be a mental thing. I must first get my emotions straightened out before the physical aspects of my world will get better.

Yes, fixing your life does begin with a change in your head—but only in grasping simple true reality (and getting you to that point is the purpose of this book). But next, you must take action *outside* your head. For real, tangible improvement to occur in your life, you must make mechanical changes within it. *First, the mechanical processes of your life must improve, and after that occurs, your emotional state will improve.*

Acquiring the "right" attitude or becoming hyper-enthusiastic are terrific, but these are states of mind, and they won't directly deliver the goods. So far, in your life, how many new mental/emotional approaches have you attempted? And how have those efforts turned out?

Accepting that simple adjustments in your mechanical world must come first is a huge step toward creating a better emotional state. If you can get control of your life's machinery so it delivers the results you want—plenty of free time, great relationships, vibrant health, and plenty of money—the good emotions will simply tag along as a by-product.

Although not as often, storms will continue to blow in, no matter how much you improve your mechanical world. Lots of time and money won't ensure that the people who love you today will continue to love you tomorrow, or that you won't get sick, or generally speaking, that your world will proceed precisely the way you want it to proceed. But then, it's unquestionable that having lots of time, extra money, and plenty of self-confidence will make unanticipated problems easier to handle. When the storms occasionally hit, it will be a good thing to be resilient and powerful.

—

But sometimes I feel so negative about things, often it seems for no reason at all. And I think about my mental state a lot, almost to the point of obsession. It would be so great to feel better about my world and myself.

Start here: Good or bad, positive or negative, emotions flow from the mechanical. It doesn't work the other way around.

There was the agricultural revolution, then the industrial revolution, and then the digital revolution. These were all clear-cut mechanical transitions, not just in economies, but in lifestyles and personal comportments. Yet there's another revolution happening right now that we don't acknowledge, one that's more of a troubling by-product than an advancement: it's the self-obsession revolution. Since the sixties, for whatever reason, we Westerners have become increasingly fixated on our moment-to-moment states of mind. We discuss, study, dictate, analyze, meditate, cajole, newscast, legislate, finger-point, and incessantly smartphone and Google it all to death. It's no wonder that almost everyone medicates themselves.

We talked earlier of this: Our self-involvement, combined

with—or maybe a result of—Digital Drug Dementia, stirs up internal dissatisfaction that prompts us to focus on what makes us feel better in the right now.

We've become obsessed with adjusting our immediate states of mind rather than in doing what we need to do to create freedom and peace down the line.

It's a self-defeating phenomenon in which the quest for freedom is subserved by the need to feel better in the moment.

–

In the big picture, we can't change the mechanics of the world to fit our perception of how things should be. Those mechanical wheels will just keep on turning, no matter our individual passions. But in the smaller picture—in our own personal lives, within our own circles of influence—we can certainly tweak the mechanisms to make things better.

I do that every day, all day long, and so can you.

In my own personal life, like anyone else, I get caught up in emotional swings. Like you, I'll have my downtimes. And once in a while, like you, I'll obsess a bit about others' behavior and the condition of the world. But I've learned these emotional dips are almost always by-products of my immediate mechanical condition. So, in the midst of a particular downtime, I get outside and slightly elevated to see that my downturn is almost a physical entity, separate from me, and often the result of some minor personal anomaly like being too physically tired, not eating correctly, or being sleep deprived. Despite my occasional slide, the world remains a beautiful place. Just remembering this simple fact immediately drives me out of my slump.

So, be a mechanic, not a psychologist: Get mechanical control first and then, I promise, the emotional control will follow.

CHAPTER 9

THE SIMPLICITY THING

Why do you repeatedly use the word "simple?"
I often think of a quote attributed to William of Ockham, the twelfth-century philosopher, which I used for the epigraph of *Work the System*. To paraphrase Sir William: "The simplest solution is invariably the correct solution." It's the tactic to take when things are fine . . . and when things are dodgy and confused. And it's a useful reminder of the mechanical truth of life that we humans tend to complicate things. We overkill by choosing a "throw the baby out with the bathwater" solution, or we get all wound up about some situation that simply can't be changed, or maybe even worse, we spend time and energy attempting to correct something that's not even a problem in the first place.

Here's how to use Ockham's law in everyday life: *When there is a decision to be made and one of the solutions is more complex than the other, and you really, really can't decide which solution to take, pick the simplest option.* And of course, many times this decision making has to do with buying something, donating time, getting involved with a group or other person, or committing to some new venture of one kind or another. If this is the case and you're not all that excited about the new idea, then "no" is the simplest solution.

We humans convolute things! It's too bad, because it's undeniable that most of our life-systems work well, and to get things rolling along better, there are usually just small adjustments that must be made. Not often is there a reason to complicate things. Ockham's simple rule of thumb works. Try it in your next decision making and see what happens.

CHAPTER 10

YOUR TASK IS TO CREATE VALUE

Before we go any further, is there a single rule of the universe that I can follow to keep me headed in the right direction?

Good for you to ask that kind of question. It shows you understand that the world functions in a formulaic way, that there are principles that work everywhere and all the time.

Without getting all woo-woo, here's something you can keep in mind: Personal freedom—meaning, among other things, lots of money and spare time—is a direct result of creating value for others. You can describe it as Karma or the Golden Rule, but in any case it has to do with addressing a mechanical reality of life here on planet earth: If you want to get ahead, no matter how efficient you are, you must deliver value to others.

In a free enterprise economy, you must do enough for someone else that they will want to pay you. In your job, when you go beyond the expected requirements, you'll find yourself moving up the corporate ladder. In your romantic relationship, improve your partner's everyday existence, and he or she will feel good about doing the same for you. With friendships, expand upon the principle of "you remember my birthday and I'll remember yours," and you'll get the same in return. And when it comes to personal health, add value to your body by thoughtfully feeding, resting, and exercising it: Do those simple things for your body, and in return it will be strong for you.

Be ardent about applying Systems Mindset rules-of-thumb like this one. Keep them front and center in your mind and apply them often.

CHAPTER 11

GOING WITH THE FLOW WILL RUIN YOUR LIFE

Is there an easy way for me to lighten up and relax?

We Westerners profess laid-back personas. Maybe it's a California thing. We're free and easy, and we tell ourselves and anyone who will listen that we're able to take things as they come. "Go with the flow" is the mantra, but it's not an effective life stance. Get right down to it and going with the flow is a silly notion because, if the flow is unmanaged, we don't have a say in how it will proceed.

Here's some sixties pop-culture heresy. It seems to me the Beatles songs, "Let It Be" and "All You Need Is Love" have done a lot of damage. There is no upward mobility or awards for those who choose to be punching bags.

Ask yourself if you really look forward to a day of external surprises.

And so I've found that those who adamantly profess to be relaxed and carefree are not that at all. *The ones who are calm are those in control of their days and who are relatively sure of what's going to happen next.* These are individuals who always seem to be in the process of building something or making things better.

These are systems specialists who constantly reach inside to improve things outside.

If there's any "flow," it's the drive within our DNA to create the future we desire. And how do we create a better future? I can't harp on this enough: We create it by seeing and then managing our machines.

Is there any reason we must be uptight in our search for control? How would that help? The application of the Systems Mindset is the antithesis of worry, because the posture is about calmly approaching the day from an outside vantage point and then quietly making constant yet thoughtful system improve-ments. It's not about overtly manhandling things.

I want you to be able to acquire more power and control for yourself, not just so you can reach your goals, but also so you can find serenity. Don't quibble about it: You can only chill out long term by controlling your machinery and thereby determining the outcomes of your life.

CHAPTER 12

BEGIN AT THE BOTTOM OF THE V

"Bottom of the V"? Whatever are you talking about?

Imagine a V as a representation of your life's progression through time. There at the bottom, nestled at the apex, is your core belief about how the world functions. Your life proceeds upward and outward from that singular point. Represented by the two expanding upward legs, your actions determine how your life unfolds, and all of your actions start with that fundamental belief, down there at the bottom of the V.

So, before proceeding let's identify your deepest belief about reality.

What is your most unshakable conviction? As an example, here's mine. More than anything else I believe the mechanisms of the world execute over time in a linear sequence: One step leads to the next step, and that step leads to the next step, etc., until the end of the process when a result is produced. This is my deepest belief of fundamental physicality. It's at the bottom of my V, and no one can change my mind about it.

So, deep down, what do you believe about how the world works? What do you think about order and disorder?

Do you think all is chaos? Or do you conclude that your existence is predetermined and that you have no control over the events of your life? Do you think we're all doomed and that life is a struggle? If the answer is yes to any of those questions, could this be the reason your life is not proceeding upward and outward in a satisfactory way? Would it be good for you to reexamine things?

—

OK, I see what you mean. But what about religion and right and wrong?

The Systems Mindset is neither supportive nor in opposition to those considerations. I'm not asking you to give up your beliefs, or suggesting what is right or wrong. I'm simply encouraging you, for a few minutes, to go one layer deeper than where you are now, below religious beliefs, political beliefs, or what you feel is proper. I'm encouraging you to dig deep to identify your most powerful conviction about how life physically functions.

Consider this: Presuming your fingers are working normally, could you, in this moment, wiggle those fingers? How certain are you that you can do this? Do it now. Did your fingers wiggle? Are you surprised they did? Of course you're not surprised. This degree of certainty is what you feel about whatever conviction lies at the bottom of your V. It's what you absolutely believe about physicality in your deepest gut. The V analogy stands on its own as your mental cornerstone of what you don't question, and you will identify and then build from this unshakable certainty. In all probability, this certainty will complement, not replace, the rest of your belief system.

Maybe your most core belief will be the same as mine or maybe you have some other absolute conviction, but whatever it is, this is the foundation you will build upon, upward and outward in the trajectory of your life.

Will this conviction empower you? Will it be congruent and contribute to your new posture of taking charge of your life? I hope so. If not, will you reexamine how you see things? In any case, it's important that you identify this core assumption now, before we go further.

Write it down here:

_____

_____

_____

_____

_____

_

OK. How should I proceed if I accept your premise that every result is preceded by a 1→2→3→4 step process and that I should spend time adjusting those processes, while always considering my deepest belief about reality?

Think about this. It's the culmination of what we've covered so far: *Successful people—the people who get what they want out of life—spend their time observing and then managing the systems that produce their results. Unsuccessful people—those who never seem to get what they want—spend their time fire-killing, constantly trying to untangle the random results of their unmanaged systems.*

This is something you'll notice as you sort things out for yourself: Where you didn't see it before, you'll start to observe defeatist life stances in some of the people around you, as well as propagated in the media. Some of these beliefs include: "The world owes me a living" or "I have a right to food, housing, happiness, money, etc." Here's another: "I'm special and the world owes me." Or, "The world is out to get me," and, of course, the classic "It's not fair!" These are horribly inefficient I'm-a-victim postures that will not only lead to disappointment, but also to outright pain for that individual and for those close by. You must avoid people who live by these insidious bromides.

And regarding what you most fervently believe: Presuming it's constructive, burn it into your consciousness and refer to it often in your decision making, because it will give you enormous self-confidence while it keeps you going in a straight line.

What to do next? Get your core belief down on paper and then start applying the Systems Mindset fundamentals in your real world. If you're still a bit unsure, you can, as I said, "Fake it till you make it." Your moment is coming soon, and I promise it will be delicious.

CHAPTER 13

THE UBIQUITOUS MISCONCEPTION

It's time again for a bit of a review. Here you'll find the fundamentals of the previous chapters combined and consolidated. If you are starting to get a feel for the Systems Mindset, this meditative chapter should enhance that feeling to something more substantial, something closer to "getting it."

–

Is there a single primary reason most people struggle financially and in their personal relationships?

Yes. *The reason so many people struggle is because they are not paying attention to the fundamental mechanics of how things work.* They think life is a complex, seething mass of sights, sounds, and events and that day-to-day survival is an epic quest; that life is unpredictable and one must be constantly on guard, waiting for the next surprise.

Considering the brass tacks of things here on planet earth, this perspective is massively inefficient. People who go through the day expecting life to execute one way, when in reality it executes another way, have concocted the perfect recipe for a life of problems. They don't know that existence is a collection of separate systems, each of which produces its own result, and because they don't see these systems of their lives, they don't manage them. And because of that, they get random bad results, not the targeted great results that are necessary for making their existences what they want them to be. That's it!

–

I understand what you're saying. You keep hammering on it. But still, it seems to me this might be just an intellectual exercise. Help me visualize how I'll be handling things once the Systems Mindset strikes.

I can see from your question that you understand the Systems Mindset but haven't yet internalized it. Sometimes, even if it makes sense intellectually, the concept can take a while to bury itself deep inside.

How will you use this new insight? Especially at work, you'll approach your tasks with this overriding filter: Can I "delegate, automate, or discard?" Because you'll know that your whole world is a collection of systems, one by one you'll analyze and then tweak each one of them to make them more efficient and to lighten the load on yourself and your coworkers. You'll first fix the most urgent dysfunctional machine and then move on to the next most dysfunctional one. You'll build new machines, too, and sometimes you'll discard ones that aren't serving you.

So many times, especially in the beginning of a Systems Mindset realignment, it really is a matter of discarding whole primary systems. But, be careful. For instance, in your romantic relationships, often it's only a matter of removing some small bad habit subsystem to please your partner. Of course, the toilet seat struggle within a relationship—whether it should be left up or down—is the classic illustration of how a small disagreement can escalate into a huge power struggle, when the mechanical truth is, it's just a tiny difference that is easily remedied by an unemotional systematic approach. (C'mon guys, it's not a big deal. When you're through, just put the damn seat down!)

And what about personal health? Visualize yourself as a robust primary system and then fix or remove any subsystems that are working against that, perhaps dropping the subsystem of obsessive overeating, or maybe modifying the informal subsystem of watching three hours of TV every night (maybe one hour is plenty). Or perhaps it's about altogether eliminating an addiction subsystem.

You'll see your separate systems and then isolate, analyze, and take action on the particular ones that must be modified or discarded. Or maybe a brand-new process will be added such as establishing a fixed methodology for staying organized at work or at home, or for getting exercise. Whatever the new addition is, you'll make sure it's a doable recurring system that will continually contribute to making things better.

You'll negotiate your world perceiving—with no doubts and most of the time with no conscious thought—the separateness and near perfection of things. No longer will you misconstrue your world as an uncontrolled flurry of happenings. Walking down the street without any overt intellectual analysis, you'll see the tree, the car, the fire hydrant, the airplane overhead, the dog, another pedestrian, your own body, each as separate machines, each part of the huge collection of individual systems that make up your world.

When you experience the joy of effortlessly carving your way through the day in this way, then you'll need no more explanation from me.

Should I give you examples of the types of decisions you can make with the Systems Mindset? No, because once you pin down your most fundamental belief and then really get a grasp of the fact that your life is a collection of independent linear systems, you'll confidently act from this new place in every instance. As you deal with your life from your new external vantage point, you'll make the correct decisions naturally.

This is not an intellectual exercise, and the learning curve is brief. This is about a better perception of the hard reality that is your existence. *When, moment-to-moment, you're seeing the visible and invisible machinery of your world accurately, you will continually adjust that machinery so it produces the results you want.* And once you start producing what you want, powerful self-confidence will arrive spontaneously. There will be no more misconception of reality—that life is a mish-mash—and that outcomes are unpredictable. Instead, without any doubts, you'll see that life, as it is, makes perfect sense.

Here's another wonderful nuance: As you move through the day with your new vision of things, you will sometimes pull back to consciously think about your world, reflecting on the separateness of things, absorbing the sheer beauty of it all. You'll assume the third-party stance, pointedly observing your own self "down there," as if you were another person, moving through time. When you occasionally take these moments to reflect, you'll remember how magical day-to-day life really is.

—

I've always thought I was randomly inserted into this confusing world, and I've learned to live with that. Will this new way of seeing things be disorienting?

Maybe your "insertion" *is* random, but what does that matter? You're here, and that's your good fortune. Yes, the "getting it" part can be disorienting at first, but in an exciting new way. Years ago my friend Chris came to me and said, "Sam, I just 'got it,' and it's making me crazy!" It took Chris several weeks to loosen up and to settle into this better way of seeing things, and so it will be for you.

As you begin seeing things differently, you'll find your life becomes fascinating. Your misconception of a world of confusion will be gone forever. Instead, you'll be as a child, intrigued with your surroundings.

Yes, it really is an enlightenment.

CHAPTER 14

THE SIREN CALL OF GOOD, RIGHT, AND FAIR

Note: These days, the issue of fairness is a political hot topic, but the controversy isn't just about determining what is fair and what isn't. The bigger question is, should the world be made to be "fair" in every instance? My position is that the world is inherently unfair, that we're all different, and since that is the case, there is no "global solution" to this natural order of things. Each of us already has an inherent "personal fairness filter," there are cultural expectations, and we have laws, so let's just leave it alone without further legal or social manipulations and punishments. Here's the part of this positioning that is especially hard to explain without sounding callous: The "fairness" thread has always weaved its way throughout our culture. It's a critical consideration and a good thing, but that doesn't mean fairness should be the prime go-or-no-go criteria for routine decision making, and taking this position doesn't mean the decision maker is "unfair." Trying to make everything fair would require external management of every nuance of life by some preselected watchdog authority, and it's a profound understatement to say that this is an unworkable proposition.

Here's the Systems Mindset mechanical take on this: If an out-side overriding criteria such as "fairness" is inserted into a decision about a particular system improvement, we've introduced foreign interference into the decision making that has nothing to do with improving that particular system. The end result of this? There will be a bad decision based on exterior criteria that introduces inefficiency, rather than improvement, in that particular system. (I'm being a bit snarky here, but maybe we should change the term "System Improvement" to "Fairness Mandate" as we intro-duce a new "fairness litmus test" to every decision?) It's so hard to explain this in a way that doesn't make me sound unfair!

—

I want to be fair and feel good about myself. How does that fit in with your dispassionate "fix the machinery first" methodology?

It doesn't fit! Look, you don't want the tail wagging the dog. Here's your ticket to nowhere: making decisions by judging whether or not your decisions are "fair" or for that matter, "right," per some external governing standard. Most people go way out of their way to be fair and good, and for that matter, thoughtful and polite. But these days it seems those qualities won't appear unless someone "does something." I find this overarching politi-cally driven nanny-state theme vexing.

Here's some equally nonsensical tail-wagging-the-dog criteria: making a decision in an attempt to feel better. Ask yourself: In get-ting a system headed in the right direction and executing efficiently, do you really believe there is a direct connection with how "good" you think you should feel and what you need to do to get that sys-tem operating efficiently? It's not that trying to be a good person is not admirable. It is, but making decisions based on subjective fair-ness, goodness, or self-gratification has nothing to do with getting a system to produce what you want it to produce. It's the same with having good intentions. Systems can't be improved via good intentions: Something has to happen! When I'm in a media interview and this good-intentions point comes up, I say, "This isn't the third grade, and your dog didn't eat your homework."

But here's the quandary in dropping fairness or goodness from your decision-making equation: There are people who will be outraged when you explain that you don't make decisions based on those criteria alone. Tell them this, and they will automatically deem you unfair and/or insensitive, or worse, a "bad person!" The correct decision-making benchmark question is this: What adjustment must I make to my machinery to get it to produce the best results? Making your decisions via this common-sense stance doesn't make you unfair, and it doesn't indicate you don't care about others.

Will you deliberately set up your machinery to "work the system," to manipulate and hurt the people around you? I hope not! It turns out that with the Systems Mindset stance, you'll naturally find yourself doing your best for others. It's a consequence of the Mindset in which you naturally add value to the people you deal with while consciously filtering out those who would drag you down. That's not being unfair; that's being smart. It's a good time to interject some lines from *Work the System*:

> In the slang sense of the term, someone who works the system uses a bureaucratic loophole as an excuse to break rules in order to secure personal gain. But winning the life-game means following the rules, for if we don't, any win is a ruse . . .

Without being distracted by short-term feel-good emotionalism, you always want to make system decisions that will propel you toward your ultimate goals without causing harm. In the short term and in the long term, taking advantage of other people is the antithesis of the Systems Mindset Methodology.

This is it in a nutshell: We're talking about mechanics here. The world is filled with people who think the better they feel about themselves, the more certain they will accomplish their goals. (Or that, if they don't reach those goals, maybe they'll score goodness points somewhere.) That's dead-end reasoning, because it's based on a false premise, one that's exactly backward. We covered this in chapter 8 but it bears repeating: *There is a connection between feeling good and accomplishment, but the accomplishment comes first while the "feeling good" tags along behind as a by-product.* It's not the other way around because the machines that produce the results don't care about how "good" you are or how "right" any particular decision might be. The systems of the world are dispassionate and nonjudgmental. They just want to produce what they have been designed to produce, and they don't give a hoot about the moral fiber of the operator. *Systems are indifferent.* This is why we sometimes see people with truly ruthless intentions in high places.

There's one thing about this, though: Good intentions notwithstanding, systems will attempt to produce what they were designed to produce, but if a person's intentions are devious— their system of operation is bucking the overall primary systems of the world— those powerful primary systems will work to neutralize the interloping system and its propagator. It may take some time but, one way or the other, manipulative people and nefarious systems will be exposed and then removed.

So, "get mechanical" about reaching your goals, but of course play by the rules while going out of your way to be generous. Remember the words of Cinderella, "Be courageous and be kind." Work on your machinery and become successful enough to become a contributor to those around you and to the world in general. *Then* you'll feel good about yourself.

CHAPTER 15

MAJOR IN MAJORS

My life is full of road blocks. I can't seem to break free . . .

Perhaps you're "majoring in Minors," not paying attention to the important mechanical apparatus of life. Could it be that you're expending time and effort in areas that seem worthwhile but have no relevance to the systems of your life that would produce freedom and life satisfaction? The "Majors" of life are too often obscured by the banality of surface reality.

I use the word Majors here to describe each of the primary responsibilities and interests of a life. And in a typical life, there are three or four, or maybe up to a half dozen.

To some degree or another, most people employ what I call "quiet courage" to get through the day. Without fanfare or complaint, they wake up, do what must be done, go to bed, and then do it over again the next day, and the next day, and on and on. In their efforts, some parts of their lives such as work, finances, family and friend relationships, health, or special interests are not optimal. You've seen this: People tend to achieve success in one or two or even three of these areas but fail miserably in the others. Don't we all know the physically fit individual who struggles financially, or the successful businessperson who has health complications?

And, there's this: Many think that if they maintain the right attitude, they'll earn the reward of freedom. Others presume one of their positive attributes will pave the way. And there are those who go for the quick fix, the big score—their particular idea is a winner, and the task is to convince others of that. And of course there is the "hard worker" who is convinced that a little more extra time on the job will do the trick.

These people are wrapped up in surface endeavors—Minors—that distract them from optimizing the machinery that would produce great results in their Majors.

Did I just describe you? If so, in this very moment, end the distractions and instead begin to major in all of your Majors. Start to coddle the systems that will produce what is most important to you. Expend your energy in quietly building and adjusting the particular machinery that will lead to freedom and life success.

—

So, what are some examples of Majors?

Defining your Majors in the context of the Systems Mindset takes some internal examination and common sense. Right now you can quickly identify what they are. Then, your next Systems Mindset effort will be to, one by one, enhance the systems that drive them, while at the same time modify or discard the systems that are dragging them down. Here are some common Majors: physical health, mental health, children, parents, love interest, career, spiritual pursuit, a personally important avocation (pilot, fisherman, athletic endeavor, etc.), nonprofit organization, hobby, politics, or the garden. There are many other possibilities, of course, but whatever your Majors might be, you want them to turn out well, and so, via the Systems Mindset, and guided by a few simple rules of the road, you'll pay special attention to the machines that propel (or retard) each of them.

Here are two examples of Majoring in Majors. (Note: They are from my personal life and are for illustration purposes only. I'm not trying to persuade you to adopt them or to see these things my way.)

First example, the Major of childrearing: What are the primary goals for the parent? In my opinion, they are to help the child to:

- grow into an adult with backbone; be someone who can forge their own way without outside assistance and who does not fall into the victim trap; become an adult who will not be a finger-pointer or the worst-of-the-worst: someone who absorbs the value others have created while creating nothing in return;

- have respect for others as well as their own selves (e.g. not contaminating the body and the mind with foreign substances, or to become preoccupied with useless time-wasters, etc.); and

- be driven to add value to others.

The three criteria comprise a whole. Each one supports the other two. What is the practical application of the parental Majors? The parent is in charge and also the role model. Every action and decision, large and small, should contribute to the above goals. And, actions and decisions that are contrary to the goal criteria are, of course, to be avoided. (For the parent, this is called integrity.)

Second example, the Major of being a business leader: In my view, there are three primary goals of leadership, all of which must be achieved and each of which crosses over and supports the other two. They are:

- to add value to the world via the creation of a product or service that people desire;

- to produce a profit for shareholders (or, in a nonprofit, to break even); and

- to accomplish the above in a sound, honorable, and nonde-structive way.*

What is the practical application for the business leader? To make sure every decision up and down the management chain meets the three criteria.

To repeat: *Once a Major is established, every action and decision that's made, large or small, should contribute to the betterment of that Major, while contrary actions and decisions are to be avoided.*

On paper, take a moment to list your own Majors and then, briefly but precisely, define each.

–

*And no, despite politicians' strident, feel-good rants, and no matter the media's wishful-thinking suppositions, the purpose of a free enterprise business is not to produce jobs. The purpose is to garner an honest profit for shareholders through the sale of a product or service that people want. In accomplishing this, jobs are created as a by-product. (And what are "shareholders"? Real people who risk their money to enable the creation of a service or product, and jobs.) And I might as well add this: A governmental effort that proclaims an intention to create jobs *and* add value will rarely succeed at both. This is because of simple human nature. Although the primary Major of government is to serve its citizens, there is another, embedded Major that is problematic: It's to spend other people's money. In any configuration, particularly government—federal, state, or local—that endeavor is fraught with inefficiency. (At this point you may ask, am I antigovernment? No, I'm not! Government is unavoidable. But I see it as a necessary evil, so I'm strongly in favor of keeping the size of it to a minimum.)

CHAPTER 16

YOUR SYSTEMS
MINDSET ANALOGY

How can I remember to apply the Systems Mindset strategy moment to moment so that eventually it takes hold? Is there a list of points I should remember? Or is there some kind of affirmation I can repeatedly recite? And do I need to remember the concepts every minute?

Don't memorize lists and don't employ affirmations. And for that matter, there's no need to make public promises to your friends and family about what you're doing (as if that would somehow force you to this better place). And don't take my word for any of this. Just go through the paces with me and then make up your own mind. And in this age of moral equivalency in which taking a firm stand is too often seen as intolerance, I challenge you to gut-believe certain principles. In fact, be judgmental. Don't be concerned about what others say you should think. *You decide what you believe.*

In any case, don't obsess about your new direction. Rather, simply keep your eyes open, observing and listening to the everyday world that surrounds you. But at the beginning, if you must do something to key into the Systems Mindset, there is a tactic you can employ with yourself. When your former my-world-is-chaos mindset resurfaces and begins to drag you down, rescue yourself with a real-world analogy. When you get distracted, it will pull you back up to your new, much more productive vantage point. In this chapter I'm going to explain the analogy concept, give you a recent example from my own life, and then finish by giving you a few recommendations.

So let's go back to the basics—the everyday physicality that you personally can't deny. Do you believe that sound comes from your throat when you talk? Can you doubt the existence of the tree that stands in the backyard? Is there any question that there are toes on your feet? And speaking of your feet, my bet is that you are totally confident that, right now, you can tie your shoes. My point is that, to give power to your analogy, it should describe a physical reality that is indisputable. You want your analogy to be gut-level believable.

A smartphone app analogy is perfect for reminding yourself of the Systems Mindset and the beauty of becoming preoccupied with System Improvement. Although all the systems of the world stand alone, a smartphone app is especially vivid in its separateness. It has a life of its own, right there on your handheld device. I came up with this particular analogy from my own experience, and maybe it will work for you. (Personally, I don't need a Systems Mindset analogy anymore because the thinking has been hardwired deep inside me for the last seventeen years, but I devised this one as an illustration for you.)

This analogy bolsters the strength of my Systems Mindset posture and suggests the level of attention I should give to every recurring system of my life: to see each as a separate entity, take it apart and examine the subsystems that compose it, and then make improvements on those subsystems.

Like any system, an app has a purpose: to create a result. The development of an app starts with someone who sees a need.

Then, often with a team, this person—let's call him or her "the owner" of the app—heads up a project to accomplish the actual code-writing. That happens, the app is released, and here is where the Systems Mindset/System Improvement analogy comes in.

If it's useful, people will use the app to add value to their lives. Then, ongoing, there will be version updates: The owner will think of a small improvement—or a user will recommend one—and then the owner will make an incremental enhancement, tweaking the code, making the app a little bit better. Usually these version updates are routine and unrushed. Other times, especially after a new release, they happen fast because a serious issue pops up.

What is the genesis of this particular analogy? Awhile back I became enamored with an app that allows me to record a voice message and then instantly send it to individuals or groups, via email. We informally named it Emailed Voice mail (EVM). It allows me to create and then deliver a voice message anytime or from anywhere, which perfectly fits my point-of-sale philosophy in which I ruthlessly take care of things *now*. Another benefit is that I can deliver a voice message without disturbing the recipient.

I really liked the EVM app, but there were problems, one of which made me want to quit using it. Periodically, as I recorded a message, the recording would unpredictably stop and I would have to begin the recording all over again. This went on for a while and became more and more of an annoyance. Finally, I delved into the app's online information and found the creator/owner. He was anxious to listen, and we went back and forth in email, trying to isolate the problem. We finally discovered the glitch and he instantly made a code modification. Within a couple of hours the new version downloaded automatically to my iPhone and my cut-off problem was fixed, never to recur.

Because of that small tweak in the code, the app became a little bit better than it was before.

This is a perfect example of system improvement, and the analogy prompts me to do things *now* and reminds me that my world is a collection of systems which I must intensely manage.

As you conjure up an analogy for yourself, remember the crux of the System Improvement approach: The end result of a single system improvement is that the primary system gets a little bit better. *Over time, relentlessly perform these subsystem tweaks—these system improvements—and the primary system will become a masterpiece. Work the system!*

I made this point earlier in a different context: Another benefit of a Systems Mindset analogy is that it illustrates the beauty of having a problem: a problem leads directly to a system improvement. In my businesses, we welcome glitches with open arms, our "red flags to betterment."

What are some other analogy possibilities? Build one around the human body, a car, a tree, an airplane, a city, a retail store, a restaurant, or a subsystem of any of these. Anything! Choose one based on solid mechanical reality and be sure it feels right for you, and then pack it around in your consciousness. After awhile, you won't have to overtly recall it, because unconsciously and consciously, you'll be seeing everything in your world via the Systems Mindset. (But it's my bet you will always remember your first analogy as a pleasant reminder of your early Systems Mindset days.)

CHAPTER 17

YOU GET TO KEEP YOURSELF

What will I have to give up once the Systems Mindset embeds itself?

Your huge jump ahead begins with a simple tweak in root thinking. Again, this is not some gimmicky self-hypnosis routine or mind game that you lay over the top of your current perception of reality. The Systems Mindset drives downward, taking you closer to how the world actually mechanically functions.

To answer your question about having to give up something, I'll ask you this question: If you become convinced you've been operating by a script that doesn't accurately deal with reality, wouldn't you happily discard that script in favor of a new approach that better addresses life as it really is? Remember, you're not being coerced here: You're going to make up your own mind.

When you "get" the gut-level Systems Mindset insight, you will be more aware than ever before. There is no way you'll want to go back to your old script.

The Systems Mindset is a perspective. It doesn't demand anything. It just is. Your new vantage point—outside and slightly elevated—will allow you to observe the precise machinery of your world, and you'll know that it's the machinery that must be tweaked.

There's nothing in these pages that suggests you should give up a hobby, go back to school, get a face-lift, quit your job, or leave a relationship. But then again, in the course of navigating your new life, you may ultimately choose to do one or more of those things. Whatever happens, you're not going to go off the deep end! Rather, you'll be thinking with more clarity than ever before.

Calmly, yet assertively, you're going to descend those steps into the basement to go to work on the machines that produce the results. Relax with it, do the work for a while, and see how it goes. Advance at your own pace, always knowing you're not going to lose you.

CHAPTER 18

YOUR PERSONAL ATTRIBUTES DON'T MATTER THAT MUCH

What? But I have a high IQ. And I'm enthusiastic, and my friends say I have a fun personality. These attributes won't help me achieve freedom?

Yes, you're right: Your attributes can help, but they won't directly deliver you what you want. You've learned that you can adjust the systems of your life to produce the results you desire, but keep in mind those systems simply don't care about you or your positive qualities.

The systems of your life are machines, not guardian angels. They won't watch over you (unless you specifically set some of them up to do that). So what about your attributes? They will be helpful in some situations but crucial in few. What doesn't matter that much? Your engaging personality, good looks, job, your friends in high places, who your dad or mom is, how much money you have, or the car you drive. Neither does your IQ, educational background, positive attitude, or even how hard you work matter that much.

What else doesn't matter? That you're on food stamps, incapacitated, didn't go to college, have a parent in prison, or don't have close friends. These are conditions, not disqualifiers for reaching your dreams.

What matters is the machinery.

Think of this in your own life: How many people do you know who have these attributes or conditions, who struggle or fail? Think of:

- successful professionals with no time;
- people with smiling faces who struggle in every area;
- stunningly attractive individuals who are enormously stressed;
- hardworking people who have toiled their entire lives but have accumulated nothing for retirement;
- parents who give 100 percent to their children but who, in turn, are disrespected by those same children;
- high school graduates who build massively profitable businesses;
- the unattractive, who have achieved everything they've always wanted, including an alluring lover;
- the reclusive, who have freedom and wealth;
- people with physical dysfunctions who are happy, engaged, and an inspiration to everyone around them; and
- employees who started at the lowest and most obscure rungs of an organization but have risen to top leadership.

Applying the Systems Mindset perspective, can you understand why the above scenarios happen? Consciously or unconsciously, the first five individuals don't see the machinery of their lives, whereas the last five do. If you asked them, could the last five explain their successes? Probably not: For most successful people, a grasp of how life-machinery operates is visceral. They don't think about it; therefore, it's invisible. And it's been my observation that most of them can't put a finger on their intuitive Systems Mindset approach.

CHAPTER 19

A BETTER YOU

What you propose is way different from how I see the world now, and I still don't "get" the Systems Mindset. I really want to, though. But when I do, I can't help but think I might slip back into my old mode of seeing things. How would I avoid that?

You won't slip back because you'll be a different person, a person who is adept at cultivating freedom, being creative, and adding value to others. Being that way feels good, and anyway, why would you want to go back to a life in which you have less control of things?

Acquiring the Systems Mindset is like getting a new pair of shoes and immediately discarding the old worn-out pair. Down the line, no matter how absentminded you might be, you won't be wearing those old shoes again. They're gone. And probably you won't even remember what they looked like. It will be the same with your former world vision: It will be gone, and you'll hardly think about it. The Systems Mindset will be your new pair of shoes.

In a very real sense, you will be a better person.

But also remember that despite the instant life improvement that occurs due to the adoption of the Systems Mindset, the adaptability of the human mind is always at the ready. For this reason, especially now, at the start, you must keep feeding yourself "good stuff" (and perhaps adopting a Systems Mindset analogy) while walking away from useless time-wasters and that which is destructive.

CHAPTER 20

IT'S A VERY GOOD THING
TO HAVE LOTS OF MONEY

But still, money is the root of all evil, right?

No, it's not, although there is a huge segment of humanity that believes it's so. For instance, in much of Western Europe, you're under general suspicion if you're in business and have done well. In many countries, wealth is no longer considered an earned reward, something of which to be proud. It's passionately coveted by many of those who don't have it, and various government entities are the great equalizers, assuring voters of the selfishness or even corruptness of people who have succeeded.

Consider this: Particularly in the United States, the vast majority of wealthy people were born here to modest means, or they came from overseas with little or nothing. Are we to believe these people lost all sense of humanity in making the journey upward? Really, does having wealth automatically indicate a character problem? I'm personally well to do, but I sure as heck am not morally corrupt and selfish. Always just barely getting by, I spent my early years scrubbing other people's toilets, digging ditches, and flipping hamburgers. With never enough money, I worked my tail off at nearly sixty separate jobs before figuring out how to break free, finally, at the age of fifty. Am I guilty of some bad act? Did I steal my wealth from someone? Of course not! What I *did* do was add value to the world and then, as a consequence, was rewarded. And as for my reward, I constantly reinvest it in the people who work for me, and my family, as well as an international nonprofit. Oh, and there's this: Once I hit the top tax margin, I must give approximately 58 percent of my income to the various government entities that demand it, and those are taxes related only to income, not taxes paid for gas, electricity, telephone service, and on and on.

So call me successful, but don't call me selfish.

Following are some reasons why being successful, including receiving a justly due monetary reward, is a very good thing.

As I illustrated above, enormous taxes are paid by those who are prosperous. In the US, in early 2016 as this book is published, the government's super-progressive tax scheme causes the top 20 percent of earners to pay over 85 percent of all income taxes, while more than 50 percent of the population pays no income tax at all.

With wealth, one can buy additional products and services beyond survival necessities. The money is recirculated. Cash flows. This means jobs.

By far, wealthy people give the most to charity.

Well-to-do people put zero drain on government social services and, in fact, fund the huge bulk of those services (including the vast bureaucratic machine that collects taxes and distributes the benefits).

Those with additional capital typically want to build more value. This means more taxes paid, more jobs created, and more new products and services produced for the consumer.

In the huge majority of cases, wealthy people are wealthy not because they took money from someone else, but because they created something of value. The free enterprise system is not a zero-sum game.

Yes, there are some bad capitalists out there. I get that. But percentage-wise, there are no more than in any other segment of society. (Greed and success are not synonyms. I'd go so far as to say that, in most cases, one is the antithesis of the other.)

In your own life, having plenty of money will give you better control—a heightened ability to decide what to do and when to do it. And yes, that personal freedom is your payback for creating value for others. Becoming wealthy is a science and an art form, an achievement of which to be proud.

CHAPTER 21

MIRACLE AT THE AIRPORT

After all this, I'm getting the sense that I haven't been able to see the forest for the trees. Am I right? If so, is there a specific place I can go where separate systems are obvious, where I can immerse myself in the Systems Mindset?

Yes, your forest/trees analogy is spot on, and your follow-up question is a good one. You're on your way to seeing the world more accurately. What will make this easy for you is that, and I've repeatedly hammered this home, *the path to your enlightenment isn't out there somewhere. It's right here, right now.* It's in your face every moment. And that's what makes the miracle invisible to most: They've taken it for granted. But you will see the systems of your life, so you will work your machinery to produce the results you desire, and be amazed at your existence. *This right here, right now is the miracle*, and even if you can't quite see it yet, you're living it as you read these words.

But having yet again said that, certain routine experiences will be especially effective at energizing your Systems Mindset.

My favorite ethereal adventure is travel. Try this: At the airport, while you're waiting to board your plane, take a deep breath, relax, and look around. With everything that's going on, notice that all the pieces work. For every waylaid traveler there will be a thousand others who will get through the incredibly complex maze to reach their destinations just fine. And consider all those airplanes in the sky at the same time. How many crashes of commercial airlines are there? Here's the statistic: Less than one ten thousandth of one percent of all flights crash. That's an incredible tally, considering the intricate assemblage of people and the complex flying machinery that must constantly challenge the incessant grip of gravity.

Consider the personnel, hardware, software, and logistics: the airport buildings, the aircraft, the maintenance and fueling of those aircraft, customer service facilities, ticketing, security, restrooms, electronic flight scheduling and displays, escalators, elevators, moving walkways, janitors, managers, shops, security personnel, pilots, and flight attendants. And this list doesn't even scratch the surface of the total separate systems necessary to make it all work.

As you sit there alongside the other waiting passengers, quietly observing the independent processes—both visible and invisible—all in motion at the same time, you can have a magical experience. As you sit alone, watching, it will be your little transcendental secret.

And what of the scores of people sitting there waiting alongside you? I guarantee that the majority of them are not gazing in wonderment, and that's because they don't "get it."

I'm enamored with auto travel, too. Think of the components of a car: the radio, door locks, cooling system, head and tail lights, exhaust treatment via catalytic converter. The engine! The turn signals, brakes, windshield wipers. Think of the transmission with its thousands of parts, and consider the tens of thousands of other separate components that work together to propel the car down the road. And while driving, note the other cars passing by, equally complex, each directed by the most incredible mechanism of all: a human body, in turn directed by a human brain. Then there is the highway system and all its intricacies. Wow!

Yes, the Southern California freeway is also one of my favorite ethereal adventures.

And think about trains. Stand by the tracks as one of these beasts hurtles by. Feel the awesome power of it. I love a train for the directed-yet-careening elegance of it.

And don't stop with human-made wonders. They pale in complexity and efficiency when compared to any aspect of nature: fields, forests, rivers, lakes, mountains, the sea, the atmosphere. Overlapping, comingling, but each separate, adding up to be the natural world we inhabit. It's a marvel, and it's right there in front of our faces.

Systems! Systems! Systems!

So what is the great "error of omission" of humanity? It's that the vast majority of us don't see the exquisiteness, the miracle. Most don't appreciate the gift.

There are a million mechanisms and daily experiences that can be isolated and then appreciated. Traveling opens up the magic with a flourish, but you can start where you are right now. Gaze around, this moment, and think of the separate components of your life; go on to consider the commingling and the cooperation—the magnificence of the dance.

Then, explain to me how all of this is an accident, and why you would ever want to go back to your former all-is-chaos mindset. Soon your appreciation of *now* will be second nature.

CHAPTER 22

YOU'LL NEVER GO BACK

Whew! Will you put all of this in a nutshell?

OK, let's go back to the root of things: It's a misconception that all is turmoil, that life is an epic struggle against adversity. The default way of the universe is order, not chaos. Look around. Maybe it's not exactly the way you want it to be, but in this moment, is the world ending?

Hardly. In fact, it's thriving. I'll say it again: You can especially see it in the natural world. It's a grand progression as life seeks to emulate itself into more complex and utilitarian forms through birth, death, and birth again, over and over.

And what about human dysfunction? It can't be denied. It's there and it's powerful, but it's a tiny slice of the whole pie. It's only front and center because it's been thrust in front of us, or it's what requires immediate personal attention. Your life is in the here and now, and it's entirely up to you to either work within your circle to make it what you want it to be, or to stand by paralyzed, fretting about the things you can't control. Your surroundings are your choice. If you don't like where you are, get up and move. No one is making you stay in this place, particularly the place in your head.

Your life can be what you want it to be if you see it for the mechanical marvel it is, and then take action.

Perfection is the norm, in this moment, everywhere, as you read these words. It's in your body, in the people around you, in the natural world. It's in your moment-to-moment ups and downs. It's there when you sleep. Just go one layer deeper and see for yourself. Open yourself up to beautiful life, as it is, and undergo your own personal enlightenment. Transcendence is in your hands.

You'll never go back.

PART TWO

MANAGING THE MACHINERY: ESSAYS

Note to reader: You've just absorbed the essentials of the Systems Mindset. Here in Part Two, the wide-ranging essay-style chapters will further enumerate these principles, but know that after you're through reading, a steady stream of additional insights and concepts will arrive spontaneously. Once the epiphany strikes, whatever the challenge, there will be no need to ask what to do next. You'll know exactly what to do.

CHAPTER 23

DISSECTION'S YOUR NAME AND REPAIR'S YOUR GAME

The first step to getting somewhere else is to establish exactly where you are right now. Measurement is key.

Let's start with the subject of health. Seventeen years ago I was very sick and headed for the most catastrophic end. But then the Systems Mindset struck, and I knew immediately what to do. Reasoning that my body is a primary system composed of chemicals—chemicals that can be measured—I broke my body down into separate subsystems via a full-screen blood test (sometimes called a "comprehensive wellness profile").

My results indicated five chemicals were out of balance, and my doctor and I immediately knew these imbalances were the cause of my horrible physical condition. With the exception of one result that pointed toward chronic dehydration, the other four indicated long-term stress was my root problem.

What was the solution? First, I learned to de-stress through yoga, meditation, and a number of adjustments in lifestyle (there's much more detail about this in *Work the System*). Second, through over-the-counter and prescription supplements, and by assertively drinking more fluids, I worked toward getting all these body chemicals back into the normal range. It took two years and a dozen more blood tests to accomplish, but I'm certain the lifestyle changes and the direct tweaking of those few bad chemical subsystems saved my life.

For the last decade and a half I've taken a full-screen blood test every six months. Results have been precisely on-target every time, not because of the supplements—I stopped taking them long ago—but because I'm now an expert in monitoring and managing my body. I eat right, exercise properly, get enough sleep, and do everything I can to ward off stress. It's a job for me, and I take it seriously, paying attention to the subsystems and then doing what must be done.

I work the system!

The repair process started with measurement, proceeded with measurement, and ended with measurement. And now that my body system is in great shape, the measurement continues.

What about *your* body? Why not do the same blood evaluation? Find out where you are now, determine where you need to be, and then tweak your subsystems so you get there.

The same methodology will work to fix relationship problems. If there is something that's not right, start by taking the relationship apart and dividing it into its separate components. Boil things down and then find the subsystem that must be tweaked. Although it might be a terrific relationship overall, a major dispute can evolve out of something as innocuous as who takes out the trash, control of the TV remote, or whether the bed is made. Or maybe it has to do with personal hygiene or a bad communication nuance. And yes, it usually ends up being some kind of struggle for control, but the isolated dispute is probably not a symptom of fundamental incompatibility and is more likely to be an isolated glitch, something that can be removed or tweaked, thus allowing the overall great relationship to thrive.

Don't throw the baby out with the bathwater.

In business,* if there is a subpar bottom line or things seem to be in constant turmoil, do the same: Acknowledge the specific problems, isolate the subsystems of the organization that are generating the troubles, and then fix things by tweaking those subsystems one by one. There's probably no need to file for bankruptcy.

Because your health, relationship, or business is having a problem doesn't mean there's an existential crisis. It simply means you're having a problem.

–

*If you want to know how the Systems Mindset works in a business, get my book *Work the System: The Simple Mechanics of Making More and Working Less*. You can find it at regular book outlets, or download it for free in PDF and/or audio at my business website, workthesystem.com.

CHAPTER 24

SEMANTICS MATTER: MAKING YOUR MACHINES VISIBLE

Your real-time vocabulary matters.

Choose the right words—what you say overtly and what you say in your head—to keep yourself on track.

Because a work, health, or relationship system can't be physically touched doesn't mean it's not there. But this system invisibility is why people don't pay attention to their systems!

The Systems Mindset will be your second-nature ability to observe the individual visible and invisible processes that make up your life; it's the art of getting outside yourself to look down on your world. To get outside and slightly elevated in order to effectively apply the Systems Mindset Methodology to immaterial processes, it's useful to use words and phrases that will make an intangible system seem physical, to posture them as physical entities that can be seen and touched.

For me, visualizing a system as a machine located in a basement evokes physicality. Here are some other terms I use: cardiovascular system, customer service system, and eating system.

Use the same tactic for your own Systems Mindset presence: Give your new protocols catchy descriptors that quickly jump to mind so you are reminded of your trajectory and goals. For instance, I use the word "coddle" to describe how I manage my machines, because the word suggests tender care for something precious. The word is always in my head, and it keeps me on track. And "outside and slightly elevated" is a phrase that is always front and center. "Point of Sale" is another good term, and I often repeat it out loud in front of my staff or friends when, because of it, I pause a conversation to take immediate action (often with the EVM function on my smartphone).*

Go back to the glossary at the end of the introduction and take a few minutes to review the definitions. Reading through the entries will be a refresher of fundamental Systems Mindset verbiage and protocol.

–

*For more information about EVM, go to workthesystem.com/evm.

CHAPTER 25

WE ARE NOT ALL ONE

The "we're all one" mantra is sixties drivel—the psychedelic-induced notion that we're all connected and therefore need to act that way. The declaration, more precisely translated, suggests that we all need to agree to the same truth and then act the same way about it.

Well, I actually do believe "we're all one." Atomic theory proves it to me, but the everyday reality is that this microscopic level of oneness is a distraction and a waste of time, because it doesn't have any effect on everyday mechanical life. But even more onerous, the obsession with oneness (and the legislated equality of outcome it suggests) erodes individual control.

How does society work best for the people in it? How is true fairness and freedom achieved? By recognizing that each of us is equal but separate, not by trying to herd everyone down the same road of identical outcome, a conformity in which there will be no upward mobility for anyone. Allow me to earn my way up! Getting everyone to conform is what is done in North Korea.

We're simply not the same, not any two of us. You're better at this, while I'm better at that. Pick a life component and make a judgment. It's OK! For a society, attempting to ensure equal outcome is a losing game, but it's a huge achievement to provide equal opportunity (and in democracies that's worked out pretty well).

And if we're going to award minority status to those whom we think deserve it, let's take the concept to its logical conclusion: Each of us individually is a minority, the minority of one. So see the separateness that is everywhere, and know it's a good thing each of us is unique.

CHAPTER 26

CLUSTERING: GUILT FREE
AND WITH A CALM MIND

Note: The following biographical chapter explains why I don't prioritize the most important component systems of my life. What you're getting here is an "advanced Systems Mindset" protocol, but it will be useful no matter your current state of fire-killing.

–

The lament is incessant: Day in and day out we quietly chastise ourselves, each of us thinking, "I need to expend less time doing this, in order to expend more time doing that." We regret not paying more attention to family, hobbies, recreating, exercising, charitable efforts, or doing some other work than the work we're actually doing. It's subtle but pervasive: the guilt-ridden conviction that we're failing to do the things that matter most, often to the point where we're feeling we're not effective people living worthwhile lives.

But here's a cognitive mind-tweak that will instantly erase that guilt, allowing you to steer yourself through a productive and satisfying day. I call it "clustering." The cluster perspective is not about the subject matter. It's about the mechanics of how the subject matter is processed and, of course, it's a simple thing.

Here it is: There is no single most important element in a life, such as "my family" or "my health" or "making money," yet we feel driven to rank these life processes in a 1-2-3 order of importance.

It's just how we tend to think, so there's no reason to feel bad about it.

Here's what happens when we rank primary endeavors: Whenever we're not immersed in what we deem number one on the list, we feel guilty, and when we *are* working on number one, we feel guilty about not attending to numbers two, three, and four. It's a losing proposition, so the best way to remove internal remorse and the personal uptightness that accompanies it is to stop ranking what is most important.

Not too long ago I was caretaker to my elderly parents. That responsibility ended when they died: first my mother, and then, eight months later, my father. I was at each of their bedsides, holding their hands when they took their last breaths.

Before they passed, my caretaking efforts included considerable time, money, and focused attention. My mother was ninety-four, wheelchair bound and declining, living in a nearby assisted living facility. I did my best to see her often, and sometimes, near the end, I would visit her several times a day. Dad was also ninety-four at the time and lived across town in an independent living community. At the same time my mother was having a hard time, Dad had a series of small strokes. In his last months it affected him enormously, and I showed up every day to help. At the very end, when he was under hospice care, I lived with him in the care facility 24/7 for three weeks.

I'm a lucky guy, because my parents survived to such ripe old ages, and every additional moment with them was a blessing. And in spending time with my parents as they were dying, it's arguable that I should have classified those efforts as "the most important." But besides the time spent helping my parents, I had other responsibilities that required my attention: other family members, my half-dozen small businesses, writing, my friends, and the routines that are necessary to stay healthy (exercise, enough sleep, etc.).

Should I have scored these other responsibilities, too, in some kind of descending order of importance?

Consciously and unconsciously, for my entire adult life up until recently, I prioritized my responsibilities and then tried hard to focus on whichever one was most important at the time. For fifteen years, as a single custodial parent, my top priority was my two children, and back then it seemed to me that my dogmatic focus was gallant, but in truth it was narrow-minded. The price I paid was constant guilt whenever I was not with my children. And when I was with them, priorities two and three were being shortchanged, and the chronic regret persisted. My composure was of ruffled uncertainty, and there was no winning the game. But that was then and this is now, and the more useful mindset I've adopted is this: In the moment, don't rank life responsibilities; cluster them.

I group my important daily system activities and treat them equally. For illustration purposes, here are my three personal "primary cluster" categories. Yours may be similar, but maybe not. If you're wondering why I have three and not two, or four, or seven, it's because, to me, three feels right:

- Contributing to my family, friends, employees, business partners, readers, nonprofit, and ad-hoc situations that come about
- Making money and wisely distributing it
- Strengthening and calming my body and mind

So what is the key stance? *The components are equally important.* This is a sensible real-world positioning because I'm dealing with the subjective. Over time, the categories are fluid, each ebbing and flowing in immediate importance, while each is always feeding and complementing the other two. This means ranking them is pointless.

Most days, I spend almost all of my time in the three components (and of course, on some days one gets more attention than the other two). Today, for instance, is a Monday morning. It's 2:00 a.m., and I'm at home working on this book, but in another half hour I'll go back to bed and get a few more hours of sleep. When I get up again, I'll handle some emails and do my daily thirty-minute personal organizing routine. After that, I'll work more on this book and then drive down to the office to see what's up and to hang out with my staff for an hour or so. In the early afternoon, it will be a visit to the gym and a good StairMaster workout. Late in the afternoon, I'll hike the river trail for an hour or so with my granddaughter Lexi. I'll be home and showered by 6:00 p.m. Then I might go out for dinner with a friend and afterward, catch a movie. Or maybe I'll stay home and sit here on the couch in front of the fire and read until 10:00 p.m. or so. Then, I'll go to bed and with no quiet, underlying guilt.

It's going to be a perfect day, loosely but deliberately choreographed, and almost all of it expended within my clusters, nearly every minute well spent.

What about my spiritual and other deep-seated beliefs? Shouldn't they be listed in the primary cluster? Are they not important enough? It's not that at all. My personal beliefs are continuous threads that weave their way through my day, like breathing, and it's the same for my certainties about how reality mechanically operates—my Systems Mindset. Some of the things of our lives don't need categorizing; they're just always there.

Since clustering happens in your head, it can be implemented instantly. And again, it's not about the subject matter, it's about how the subject matter is processed. Identify the most important system elements of your life on paper,* declare them equal in importance, and then spend most of your day focusing on the system elements of each. Don't keep score. The cluster components will smoothly intertwine, and the results will be well balanced and satisfying.

It's all good!

What is clustering's exquisite bonus? A nonfrenetic mind. Here's a favorite quote from James Allen's book, *As a Man Thinketh*: "A man becomes calm in the measure that he understands himself as a thought-evolved being . . . and as he develops a right understanding, and sees more and more clearly the internal relations of things by the action of cause and effect, he ceases to fuss and fume and worry and grieve, and remains poised, steadfast, serene."

So, no more prioritizing! Instead, cluster. And through the day, as you add value to the various important segments of your life, there's no guilt, just calm satisfaction.

⁓

*In these pages I've several times mentioned putting things down "on paper" and can suggest a protocol for that. I go into great detail about business documentation in *Work the System*, but briefly, here are three written documents you might consider putting together for your personal life.

The first is your Strategic Objective. It's an enhanced personal mission statement, limited to a single page. It describes who you are and where you're headed, including your goals and how you intend to reach those goals, as well as your strengths and weaknesses, etc. The second document lists your Operating Principles.

These are guidelines for what I call "gray-area decision making." This document lists your specific root beliefs about life and how you intend to apply them. It's maybe two or three pages long and may include thirty or so separate points.

For business, I recommend a third document series called "Working Procedures." Occasionally, they are useful in personal life.

For more information regarding these documents as they pertain to business, read chapters 10 and 11 in *Work the System*. For examples of the documents applied to a personal life, go to thesystemsmindset.com/documents.

CHAPTER 27

AUTOMATE, DELEGATE, DELETE

Use the title of this chapter as the filter for many of the decisions you make, especially at work.

If you're going to quickly get out of the middle of things and gain a truckload of personal control, you must be sure you're headed in a single direction, not helter-skelter, all over the place. It really does boil down to picking the correct road and then traveling down it efficiently, and a great way to assist that effort is to pass every decision through this "task filter."

To reinforce the concept's validity, think about the opposite tactic: doing every task manually or doing them all yourself, or accepting every burden that shows up on your doorstep. And yes, it's especially about work, but it's also about relationships and health.

Automating and delegating can be combined. For example, my strength coach at the gym, Scott, guides me through my twenty-minute high-intensity training session. The automating part is simple: I just need to show up as scheduled. The delegating part is giving control to Scott. Here's an illustration of the effectiveness of it. Just a week ago, as I was writing this chapter,

Scott put me on a horizontal leg press machine and loaded it up with tremendous weight. He said, "I want fifteen" (repetitions). The weight was more than I had ever dealt with before and at the fourth repetition, gritting my teeth through the pain, I told him I couldn't do even one more. He firmly balked and persuaded me to continue. I plugged along—slowly, agonizingly—somehow getting the full fifteen. For a few minutes afterward, I stumbled around in exhausted stupor as I asked myself where those other eleven repetitions could have possibly come from. But the answer was simple. I had given management of the process over to Scott. Even though I was the one who had met the challenge, I had effectively delegated the management of my performance to someone else.

And what about "deleting?" Maybe the simplest illustration is to imagine you're in a romantic relationship that is not turning out to be what you had hoped it would be, while the other person thinks it's going fine. Rather than try to make it work when you know in your heart it never will, use the "delete" part of the formula to simply end it. The alternative is a frustrating, wasteful expenditure of energy for both of you (and of course it will ultimately end anyway, just further down the road). Being able to decisively walk away from a dead-end scenario like this is a powerful personal attribute.

I like the automate-delegate-delete formula because it simplifies decision making. We humans, as I've said, like to complicate things.

There's one other thing. Know that you already delegate and automate all day long. Truth is, although you don't know it, you're really, really good at it. As an example, I'm going to give you a Systems Mindset vision that you will not be able to shake. Be forewarned that it *will* embed itself in your head. It has to do with a daily ritual that you've taken for granted up until now. Here it is: In the morning after you wake up, shower, dry yourself off, hang up the wet towel, get dressed, and then go about your day's activities—have you ever thought back about that wet towel, hung up and drying, back there in your bathroom, requiring zero attention or additional input from you?

There is significant importance here if you can see it: This towel-drying system is a perfectly automated machine that requires no maintenance or management, and it's 100 percent successful every single time. Hanging your towel up to dry is maybe the ultimate act of automation, one that you haven't thought about until this moment. You hung up that wet towel, and the drying system flawlessly executed over a period of time, to completion. With one small initial effort, you made it happen! And now that I've laid this out for you and you've considered it, I guarantee that your future towel-hanging will be accompanied by the comforting thought that "this is a wheel that will turn to completion all by itself with zero additional input from me!"

But this is just about a towel! All through the day, there are many more instances of this hands-off delegation/automation that you haven't thought about from the outside and slightly elevated stance. How about the refrigerator that keeps your perishables fresh no matter what you're thinking or doing during the day; the clothes washer in which you load the clothes inside, add soap, and then walk away, not thinking even once about the complex system execution happening over the ensuing hour or so. And of course, there's the clothes dryer: It's the same thing. Think about the myriad other machines that are working for you in the background, machines that you activated but then execute to completion entirely by themselves. Until this moment, it's my guess that you haven't given a second thought to any of them.

It will be good for you to casually reflect upon these small processes from the Systems Mindset standpoint—and not just today, but always. It will keep your head straight.

You're already a master at delegation and automation! Now that you see you're already good at it, consciously doing more of it will be easy.

CHAPTER 28

TEXTING ISN'T ENOUGH

Let's poke a hole in Ockham's law, that the simplest solution is usually the correct solution.

More and more, general one-on-one communication is devolving into the texting mentality: it's too short and concise, too interrupting. Let's join together to fight this slide.

So what is the Ockham's law exception? It's this: In work communications, yes, leave out ongoing chatter about nonbusiness matters. Please do get to the point, but don't play the robot by taking communication protocols to ultra brevity, to the brink of rudeness. In the midst of our too-busy days, we can sacrifice a few seconds to being friends, can't we? Prattle on a bit about your life, even if we've just connected for the first time. Tell me some small thing about yourself, and then ask me about me, *then* let's get on with things. For a great relationship, silence is not always golden. Keeping things simple is a good rule of thumb, but let's be reasonable.

It's OK. It will only take a few additional seconds.

Especially germane to work, but also relevant to personal communications, here are nine tips for sending and receiving texts, email, and voice mail that you can implement instantly.

Text only for immediate concerns and for family: Anyone under sixteen will roll their eyes at this. Why be hard-nosed about texting? Because you don't want to be interrupting other people for routine matters, and you don't want to encourage others to interrupt you about something that can wait. It's a good thing to be able to focus for more than ten seconds at a time! If your issue can wait, let it wait in my email inbox, and I promise to get to it soon. Don't get sucked into a frenetic texting protocol that in all likelihood has been adopted by every single teen you know and is quickly inserting itself into adult communications. (Most teens don't even have email addresses, and because they hardly ever talk to each other, neither do they set up or use their smartphone voice mail boxes.) My tactic is to respond to unsolicited nonurgent texts with email. And when senders don't get the hint, insistent that I join their texting mania, I explain that I reserve texting for urgent and family matters only. Here's a great book regarding focus and concentration: *Flow* by Mihaly Csikszentmihalyi.

Point of Sale (POS): If you're going to communicate, send your message *now* (most often email and voice mail, not text). Why? Because POS is almost always the most efficient way to do things. The person on the receiving end will appreciate it, while you'll get the matter off your plate. Does this mean you should respond to messages right this second? Yes, if possible, but this doesn't mean you should check your messages every two minutes. (See the next point.)

Be militant about protecting your focus time: On your smartphone, don't constantly check for messages! It annoys the people around you while it adds a degree of mania to your own personal composure. But you know that already, don't you? Check for messages every couple of hours or so. Who's the boss, you or that little electronic device? And on your laptop, turn off the incoming message notification. Do you have an office door? Maybe close it more often.

The silent treatment: Failure to respond to a message is rude. The perception is that you are not paying attention, are overwhelmed, and/or simply don't care. If in a given situation you're not sure if you should communicate, you should communicate. (This guideline, of course, doesn't apply to nonsolicited sales messages).

Think it through: Thoroughly read messages you receive before responding. And as you compose a message, double-check it carefully before sending. Are there grammatical errors? Does it make sense? Your message is you!

Quality and quantity: At work and in personal life, emphasize quality *and* quantity. If there is steady communication—generally email and voice mail, not text—quality will evolve. But note: The quantity aspect has more to do with frequency than with volume of content. Rambling dispatches that contain more information than necessary, or messages that keep repeating the same detail, are a waste of two people's time. At work, the voice mail medium is particularly susceptible to fatiguing, inefficient messages. But then, often a voice mail message is much faster and more meaningful than an email, and sometimes a thirty-second voice mail will deliver a more effective message than a ten-minute-to-compose email.

Study your speech: A potent learning technique is to record yourself in a conversation and then review your part of that conversation. For most of us there is incongruity between how we think we sound and how we actually sound. Quirks, bad habits, and outright dysfunctions can be instantly eliminated if you become aware of them.

The above self-analysis will encourage you to deepen your voice and promote conciseness; to drop the colloquialisms "yeah," "yup," and "ya know." Using slang like this will give the impression that you are unprofessional and uneducated. Other common verbal faults include not pronouncing "Gs" at the end of words, endlessly interjecting "umms," and overusing legitimate words such as "so" and "like." And you'll want to eliminate some tired pop idioms such as "I'll let you (do, explain, take care of, etc.) it," "I mean," "to be honest," and "no worries." As you listen to yourself, maybe you'll hear other words you'll want to use more sparingly/appropriately such as "absolutely," "exactly," and "amazing." And perhaps reconsider use of the cloying "I'll reach out (to so and so)." If you're a waitperson in a restaurant, don't refer to a male/female couple as "you guys." It's too bad that so many good words and phrases have devolved into throwaways, their original meanings neutered via colloquial overuse/misuse.

Don't up-talk!: This is the valley-girl solecism of ending sentences with an upswing in tone. It's amusing and annoying to hear, especially when employed in sentence after sentence. Everything sounds like a question.

Do what you say you're going to do: For instance, if you commit to send information to someone by a specific date, do it and do it on time. If something comes up and you can't meet the deadline, inform the other party before the deadline. But of course, this is not just for email, text, and voice mail messages, it's for everything you do.

Those are mechanical and pointed recommendations, and I believe Sir Ockham would approve.

CHAPTER 29

MAKE POINT OF SALE
AN OBSESSION

The POS term was coined in the retail industry and it encapsulates the goal of getting the wheels rolling now, in the right direction, and at high speed. And the term insinuates the converse: the elimination of wheels that are rolling in the wrong direction. But there's more to the posture than promoting efficiency; it's not just about getting things done. We'll get to that.

In chapter 16 I explained the importance of packing around a systems analogy, and I gave an example of one I created. Again, the purpose of a Systems Mindset analogy is to keep yourself on track. Here's an "analogy game" that I have developed over the past couple of years, one that I use in presentations. Note the hyper-specific details, added so the visual impression settles firmly in the back of the mind.

—

Wheel Turning

I play an imaginary game in which I'm standing in the middle of a large open, flat grassy field. It's a beautiful early morning in June, the sun is rising, and I've just arrived. I've located myself at the center of a circle (yes, my circle of influence). From where I stand, it's exactly half a mile to the outer perimeter. I'm relaxed, thinking and watching, looking outward and taking it all in, scanning 360 degrees around. In one direction, in an outward expanding pie shape with me standing at the pointy end, are the requirements of my various businesses. At another angle, the expanding cone contains my health and body maintenance, and in another direction are my friend/family relationship responsibilities. I stand there, looking out and all around, energized, thinking about the tasks I must accomplish. Then, those tasks materialize in front of me in the form of a half dozen large, wooden wheels. I call them "task wheels." These wheels represent the undertakings I want to accomplish, or at least begin to accomplish, today.

The wheels are five feet in diameter and they surround me, each one standing up on edge with the twelve-inch-wide rim facing me, which means the rim on the opposite side is facing out. I can see over their tops, looking outward toward the edge of the circle. (If someone were to look downward from directly above it would look like the blossom of a flower, with me standing at the center.) Each wheel is light-framed and well-constructed, with wide wooden spokes holding it all together. (Imagine a water wheel.) These task wheels are just standing there, surrounding me, immobile and balanced on their rims, each a mere arm's length away, and it's my job to firmly push those task wheels, one at a time, to get them rolling away, out of my immediate proximity, each moving outward through the middle of their respective cones and toward the edge of my circle where, once crossed, the tasks will be complete.

I'm passionate about the automate-delegate-delete methodology so, one by one, I firmly shove the task wheels off, and they trundle away. I pause for a moment to watch the last one of this early morning batch move away but then promptly summon up more wheels. As they materialize next to me, one by one, I quickly push them off, too. Soon, there are dozens of wheels rolling outward, each within their respective "cone" and each moving away at a different speed. Some will reach the perimeter within five minutes; others will take days, or even weeks or months.

It's a moving, active game, and I like being at the center of it.

This analogy is about massive accomplishment, and the wheels represent the tasks that must be done in order to make that accomplishment happen. Whether I'm paying attention or not, when a rolling wheel reaches the outside perimeter of my circle, that task is complete.

This is a fun game because I feel control and satisfaction. At any time I could walk away, but I choose to stay.

If I didn't push the wheels away toward the perimeter, they would accumulate until I was hemmed in behind dozens of adjacent wheel rims. But that never happens because I stay ahead of things, dispatching the wheels as soon as they materialize next to me. I'm good at this game, so it's always open and clear around me as I eagerly await the next wheel's appearance, ready to instantly push it away, too.

I push, push, push, and the wheels lumber away in their prescribed trajectories. There's constant movement out there the wheels bobble away, but my involvement with that ongoing movement is minimal. Most often, other people guide the wheels to completion, out there in the various cones. I'm the instigator, not the doer.

As the leader of my businesses, and in my personal life, my job is to envision tasks and then, whenever I can pull it off, quickly give those tasks to other people to complete.

And if I just stand there, indifferent, without conjuring up new undertakings? Then no wheels appear, and it's just me, standing idle in the middle of a field.

So back here in my tangible world, my job is to decide what tasks are to be done and then, one by one, to immediately get them in motion so they can be completed ASAP. I conceptualize those task wheels, either from my own imagination or, often, from the suggestions of others. My job is to decide what must be done, not to do the work. Whether it's an early morning four-hour writing session (like this one), or, later, a quick meeting with my accountant at 8:30 (there are some statistics that I need her to compile), coffee with one of my business partners (at 10:00), my weekly two-hour massage (this afternoon at 1:00), taking my daughter Jenny and my two grandchildren to dinner (tonight at 6:00), or a call later this evening to my friend Sue up in British Columbia who is recovering from major surgery, I keep pushing those wheels outward.

Push. Push. Push.

In the game analogy, are there ever any wheels that spontaneously materialize, unsolicited by me? Not often, because a long-term consequence of the game is that there is little fire-killing in my life. I carefully manage the processes of my existence so they produce only the results I want.

This wheel-turning analogy is my contrivance. It feels right to me. Use it for yourself or devise one that suits you better, then embed it in the backroom of your consciousness. Perform POS all day long.

—

Snow Removal

Yesterday, snow fell steadily and it blocked the long driveway to my house here in Bend, Oregon. So last evening, because snow is never lighter than when it first falls, my wheel-pushing consisted of two hours of snow shoveling in the dark. I love this work, and always do it myself. There were sixteen inches of fluffy, light powder, and I worked steadily. The process turned into a physical, meditative prayer to my recently deceased father, and as I plugged along I thought back to long ago, to another dark, cold nighttime driveway choked with snow. Last night I was my eleven-year-old self, way back there in the tiny village of Port Leyden in remote upstate New York. It was 1962, and I was bundled up in the darkness there, next to Dad, in the still, quiet cold. The snow was still falling. We each had our shovels and as we quietly worked alongside each other in the faint glow of a single streetlight, there was only our heavy breathing and the muted scrape, scrape, scrape of our shovels as we incrementally moved the deep white blanket of fluff off the driveway and up over the towering snowbanks. There, in my childhood driveway, in the heart of the Tug Hill–Black River snow belt, the depth of a new snowfall was often more than four feet.

There was a mechanical job to be done *right now*, before the weather warmed up and the snow got heavy. Dad envisioned these snow-removal projects and always recruited me. We'd bundle up, exit the house into the storm, and then we'd hit it hard. The two of us were steady and relentless, and we churned ahead silently and thoughtfully. Sometimes it was a three-hour epic. Those raw, wheel-turning quests were enormously satisfying, and at the end of a job, exhausted, we would quietly stand together on the porch for a moment and take pride in what we had accomplished: We had carved a perfect path through the onslaught of the storm. Then we turned around, stomped the snow off our boots, and withdrew back inside the house where it was always warm and cozy.

Dad wasn't physically with me last night—he passed away one year ago—but the "right now" wheel-turning was no different, and in my prayers I thank him for teaching me about getting a job done immediately and precisely, to "get on with it," and for showing me that true satisfaction is found in just that.

These days, in my work, the major wheel-pushing is done by me, with the legwork handled by my staff (automate-delegate-discard). But within their own various realms, my managers are wheel-pushers, too, and with their firm nudges their business task wheels also continuously roll outward. For each of us there are numerous wheels rolling away, some in sequence and some simultaneously, and each at a different speed, but every one of them was launched quickly via POS protocol.

And for me, beyond the satisfaction of watching it all unfold, the payoff includes the personal luxury of having lots of time: to write, to read, to be with my friends and my family, to travel, to create more machines, and to do whatever I feel like doing.

I said it earlier: Your attitude, IQ, personal history, energy level, or how hard you work aren't that critical. In creating freedom in your life, the moving wheels of the machines are what matter. It's important that those wheels are conjured up in the first place and then quickly pushed forward. This is the vision I carry every minute of every day. Is it tedious? No. It's a creative delight.

I mentioned at the beginning of this chapter that there's more to POS than efficiency. It's deeper than that because it affects everything in a life, right down to root beliefs. POS is how I handle all my tasks, spending time in the center of that field, nudging those wheels outward. It's an ongoing self-declaration of life control.

If your goal is freedom, it's your job to create task wheels and then push them outward *now*. For starters, perform this POS thought process within the context of your current work and personal life, and don't turn the big things of your world upside down (not yet, anyway). Get a feel for how the approach works, *be patient but deliberate, do the right things in the right sequence, and do them now.* Get good at it, and then watch with calm satisfaction as your life comes under control and your circle expands.

CHAPTER 30

PRIME TIME

Prime time has two components, Biological Prime Time (BPT) and Mechanical Prime Time (MPT). The two have little in common, but they go together well.

BPT is the period of the day when you're the most energized, a stretch of time lasting six to eight hours in any twenty-four-hour period. Like many people, my BPT begins the moment I wake up, and I'm out of gas by early afternoon. BPT is the segment of the day I'm strongest and smartest, so it's ruthlessly devoted to accomplishment, at my work mostly. There is no more effective period for me and I never fritter it away.

Others have a BPT that begins in late afternoon and stretches into the early morning hours, and there are those whose BPT lies somewhere in between.

Determine when yours occurs and then never waste it. These are the hours you assert control, to do what you need to do to create even more of it. You are better during these periods. Your thinking is sharper and your actions more adroit. Your effectiveness will be triple what it is during your non-BPT hours.

For me, what is wasted time in those hours? It's exercise, reading, going for a hike, hanging out with friends. Those are important endeavors, but none contribute directly to what I need to do to gain more control and freedom in my life. And what do I *do* during my BPT to advance my own long-term control and freedom? I do my MPT tasks. (We'll get to that.)

And what about reading, routine chores, exercising, and hanging out with friends? Try to limit these activities to non-BPT hours, although there will be occasions when you have to be sharp during these less-than-optimal times. If my BPT is in the early morning and there is some critical personal requirement in the evening, how do I energize myself so I'm not sleep-walking my way through that important task? I find a way to take a nap in the afternoon.

Using BPT wisely will quickly jump you ahead. Protect it and parse it out carefully. Be jealous of it and do not fritter it away.

How do you know when your BPT occurs? If you're not a heavy caffeine user, you already know when it is, but if you're a first-thing-in-the-morning coffee drinker you may not know when it occurs because the caffeine creates a false BPT. (You could call it Chemical Prime Time.) That's a tough thing, because for the caffeine-addicted the only way to discover true BPT is to quit, and that can be an onerous quest. (I've written a three-part blog series on beating caffeine addiction. Go to workthesystem.com/caffeine.)

If you're a heavy alcohol consumer, you're probably also a caffeine drinker. I recommend you find a way to control the alcohol consumption, because if you don't, your life is going to have problems way beyond figuring out when your BPT occurs. Reduce or eliminate the alcohol first and then deal with the caffeine and any other addictions.

MPT is very different from BPT. MPT is not about your most effective time period, it's about what you *do*. MPT is comprised of the mechanical tasks that you have to accomplish that will expand your personal control and freedom. These are your one-time machine-building efforts that make it possible for you to "make more and work less."

Here are some examples of my own MPT: R&D, strategic meetings with business partners and managers, working on my next book, writing blog posts, interviewing people who will work for me, speaking to groups, and doing interviews with the media.

Combining BPT and MPT is the perfect synthesis as you perform your machine-building tasks during the time of day when you are the most powerful.

CHAPTER 31

YOUR MIND CAN BE A BAD NEIGHBORHOOD

Thinking is a system, and in the down times it can be a scary thing to endure. When uncontrolled negative thoughts start to cycle one after the other, it's like finding yourself in a bad neighborhood, knowing for sure that your best bet is to quickly get out of there, to a safer part of town.

Being able to get out of your head at a moment's notice is an essential step toward finding freedom and peace. You want to develop the ability to step outside and slightly above that streaming video that is your thinking process, knowing in your gut that the thinking itself is an isolated system that can be directed. Do that, and you're on your way to effectively managing your own little slice of reality.

Are freedom and personal peace even possible? Not completely, because everyone has a cross to bear (including yours truly, of course). For you, like everyone else, it's going to be impossible to permanently stay out of the bad neighborhood, but there is no question that when you find yourself there, you can quickly escape by taking a cognitive approach that jives with reality.

And remember this about the thinking process: The brain is not capable of processing more than one thought at a time.

Thinking is linear, with one thought following another, relentlessly. You can subconsciously multitask (e.g., driving a car, walking and talking, etc.), but you simply can't multitask your overt thinking. Thinking is strictly a one-at-a-time endeavor, and the proof of this is to try having two conversations at once.

But, although sequential, the thinking system is quickly malleable. So knowing this, scrutinize your mental deliberation by getting outside of it, watching it, and then reaching in and directing it. If your thoughts begin to go down the road toward the bad neighborhood, interrupt them and get them out of there.

If you don't control the content of your deliberation, who or what controls it? Our peer group, TV, electronic gadgets, a guru? Or maybe it's some feel-good menu of life that is more wishful thinking of how you think things should be rather than how they actually are. Carefully steer what happens in your head (and promise me you won't mess up your miraculous thinking mechanism with state-of-mind-changers).

Visualize your thinking as a streaming video in which it's your job to control the flowing images as they, one by one, pass by your consciousness. Watch your thinking happen and consider those thoughts as guests: Who will they be; how long will they stay? Do you want them to be there at all?

This ability to watch your own moods and emotions from an outside location really is the simple solution. It's no more complicated than being able to mechanically reframe your thoughts, to change the channel, so to speak. At home alone on the weekend, lonely? Go see a movie, clean the house, take a nap, eat something healthy, go shopping, call a friend. Take the mechanical approach to channel your emotions into a better place. Boring but true: It's *that* simple.

Ask yourself: Am I going to assertively direct the content of my thought processes or not? And take this expression home with you: Sometimes my mind is a bad neighborhood, and when it is, I need to get out of there.

CHAPTER 32

DEAL KILLERS AND
THE MAIN MACHINE

The Main Machine is you. You're a primary system, an enclosed entity made up of numerous spinning wheels, all contributing to the singular purpose of that entity, this is, to accomplish a goal.

You're precisely engineered, perfectly equipped to choose objectives and then adjust your output in order to reach them.

And whatever your goals might be, of course it makes sense to drop any behavior that hinders their attainment. This chapter is about deal killers: the things you might be doing or might not be doing that could erase the accomplishments you've managed to secure (or are about to secure). I also list some routines for maintaining and strengthening your "main machine."

Here's a pragmatic overview—the problems and their solutions—of three common deal killers. It's a numbers game, and it's my guess there's at least one that is relevant to you. (And if not, then certainly to someone you know.)

First, there's chemical addiction. If you have one, you must find a way to defeat it. There is help out there, and a quick Google search will tell you where to find it. Interesting that at Centratel, where we relentlessly drug test, it has become increasingly hard to find job applicants who are not drug users. It's become worse in the last year as marijuana has become legal in Oregon and therefore socially legitimized. So, over the last several years, as we've watched the accelerated acceptance of chemical state-of-mind "adjusters," we've informally worked with alcohol and drug recovery groups in our Central Oregon region in order to find "clean" job applicants. These are people who have been to hell and back and don't care to return. (See workthesystem.com/clean for more specific information.) This isn't a complicated or nuanced recommendation: If you're searching for true freedom, you must defeat any addiction to drugs or alcohol. I challenge you to live your life cold turkey.

And, second, there's sleep deprivation. How boring to hear yet again that most of us don't get enough sleep. But it's true. The human body requires a certain amount of sleep in each twenty-four-hour cycle. Getting enough of it is not something you do only when you have the time. It *has* to happen or things will go bad. Obsess about it, fight for it, and do whatever it is you have to do to get enough. And please don't be one of those people who wears their sleep deficiency as a badge of courage.

Cut back your caffeine intake, and you'll find yourself naturally getting more shut-eye. Generally speaking, chemical sleeping aids are a bad idea. And go for the dreams, because when you dream hard—it usually happens at the end of your sleep cycle—you're experiencing delta sleep, which is the deepest and most rejuvenating phase of the cycle. Here's my favorite book on the topic: *The Promise of Sleep* by William C. Dement. It's an older book and a classic.

Third, coddle and challenge your physical body, your "main machine." It's the ultimate primary system of your existence—the vehicle that carries you around—your special endowment. Incredibly complex, it wants to perform well for you, so do what you have to do to keep it strong and resilient. I'll spare you the lecture about how the body affects the mind and vice-versa, because of course you already know that.

Taking proper care of the body is a moment-to-moment quest. Following are details of my personal stay-well master system. The commonality among the various segments is that they are all "mandatory preventive maintenance" efforts, the moves I *have* to make whether I want to make those moves or not.

Cardio. With only a few brief pauses, I've been at it since I was twelve. The prolonged stress of cardio keeps all the systems of the body strong. Each week, I do one high-intensity interval workout, plus an additional two or three that are moderately stressful. My preferences are road and mountain biking, mountaineering, and cross-country skiing. I mix it up, though, depending on the season, with a fallback to the StairMaster if no other options are available.

Resistance Training. In the gym, once a week with my coach, I work with heavy weights in an intense twenty- to thirty-minute session, taking each muscle group to failure, and then a bit beyond. It's an anaerobic/aerobic ordeal that renders me useless for two hours, and then requires three to four days for full recovery. It took twelve weeks to adjust to the stress of it, but now these sessions are the cornerstone of my week. In just a few months I added ten pounds of muscle. Google or ask around about High Intensity Training (HIT). Consider employing a hard-ass trainer, one who won't treat you like a delicate buttercup. If you live in Central Oregon, you'll want to use my coach, Scott. Email us at info@systemsmindset.com and we'll give you his contact information.

Yoga. Through the years, our muscles and tendons contract. Yoga counteracts this incessant tightening. I like Bikram Yoga, which conforms exactly to the Systems Mindset Methodology: The standard routine of twenty-six postures is precisely choreographed, so you know what you're going to get in each ninety-minute class, no matter what studio you attend. And, the postures are exactly sequenced from easy to hard, so you won't get hurt and you get maximum benefit. I've been doing yoga for seventeen years and attend a session every three to four days. This is an essential routine if I am to be injury free. Go to workthesystem.com/bikram to read a post I published about it. There's one authorized Bikram studio here where I live, operated by my friend Susie. You'll find it easily enough. If you live elsewhere, Google "Bikram Yoga." Per Wikipedia, there are about six hundred studios worldwide.

Chiropractic. I like a solid tweaking, where I can feel my bones realign. After the adjustment, I always feel looser, more relaxed. I schedule one adjustment per month. Dr. Michael Toby is very good, and he happens to be a commercial tenant in our building in Bend, Oregon.

Meditation. Read the classic *Full Catastrophe Living* by Jon Kabat-Zinn. It's a great place to start. Like my yoga practice, I've been meditating for seventeen years, and I began with a six-class course, spread over six weeks. The best part of meditation is that you get a break from the incessant mental noise, giving your problem-solving mind a break. At first it's a challenge to slow the surging freight train of thought, so be patient. I meditate off and on through the day, in bits and pieces, sometimes for just a minute or two at a time. I also do it every night before I sleep, and with my own homegrown routine, counting my slow exhales from one to five, I fall asleep within twenty seconds. Google, "Mindfulness Meditation."

Deep-Tissue Massage. I need it on a weekly basis because of my intense exercise routines combined with long hours on the computer keyboard. Here in Bend, I employ Kirsten, who is expert at going deep to find emerging problems. Search "relaxation deep-tissue" and/or "integrative/therapeutic massage." If you're local, contact us at info@systemsmindset.com, and we'll put you in touch with Kirsten.

Diet and Overall Health. Not too long ago, I completed the Unicity Transformation program. It's a semi-intense, coaching-based three-month course focusing on proper nutrition, but also it's about lifestyle, including exercise and stress reduction. There's careful customization for the individual. The client is held accountable, and there is detailed results tracking. It revolves around a weekly one-half-hour telephone training session with a Unicity coach. With my dietary and exercise routines tweaked to fit, I know exactly what my body needs. Now at 170 pounds, I'm not a big guy, but over the twelve weeks of the program I lost twenty-five pounds of fat. Combined with the simultaneous gain of muscle due to my HIT gym workouts, I dropped my body fat from 22 to 10 percent. The Unicity program is systematic, perfectly aligned with the Systems Mindset Methodology. You can find an overview of the program at defineyoury.com. For more information or to enroll, contact my office at info@systemsmindset.com.

CHAPTER 33

OBSERVING THE FAMILY SYSTEM

If you haven't traveled to a third-world country and lived there for a while with locals, consider finding a way to make it happen. My most memorable exotic family experiences have been in China, Pakistan, and Azad Jammu Kashmir.

Live for a while with a local small-town family, and for starters—for the sheer culture shock-value of it—I recommend a decidedly different culture, such as in the Near or Far East. With your new friends, sleep in their house, hang out with them during the day, share meals, talk to them about their lives, and listen to their aspirations and fears and their rants and raves, and all the while, if you're like me, be thankful that some of them speak English.

In late October 2005, just after the devastating Pakistani and Kashmiri earthquake, I was in Pakistan and Azad Kashmir, on my own, doing relief work and freelance reporting. It was a down-and-dirty time, horrible for the tens of thousands of families who were homeless (in the truest sense of the word, living in squalid tent camps that were spread throughout the region). The physical conditions for these refugees was unspeakable. Their mental torment was compounded by the high death toll, which included a disproportionate number of children who were caught in nonreinforced stone and concrete school buildings that collapsed. During my stay there, I wrote the following:

–

Twelve time zones removed from my home in Oregon, in remote northern Pakistan, where the family is the heart of the culture, there is fascinating contrast to our Western norms. The social system is inflexible. All marriages are arranged, with the majority first-cousin to first-cousin. The religion is exclusively Islam, the structure starkly patriarchal. The average family includes five children. The back-country Pakistani family is inviolate; its mandates are inarguable, and the rigid rules are the hub of all. There's no violation of the tenets of the clan. The extended family is huge, yet, because of marriage protocol and cultural expectation, tightly knit. Everyone works hard. Everyone prays. There is no unraveling of the threads that stitch things together.

In the remote region I am visiting, there is little interest in geopolitics or the social concerns with which we Westerners belabor ourselves. Is this good or bad? That's not the point of this chapter, so we'll let that part go.

Magta Khan and his family live in the foothills of the Karakoram Mountains of the Gilgit-Baltistan district (formerly known as the Northern Areas) of Pakistan. Their tiny village is at a high elevation and is only accessible by foot. It's an agricultural life, and the entire family, including children, toil from spring through fall to put aside stores for the long, hard winters that, in Khan's family's case, include up to eight meters of snow. This means the family, for literally months at a time, does not venture out of the house even to visit nearby neighbors. The snow is too deep. I ask Khan, what do all of you do with yourselves over those long, dark months in your house? We talk and pray, he says. Do you get bored? No, he says, we have lots to talk and pray about. My claustrophobic Western brain recoils, but then I remember that uncomplicated systems work best, and I understand that the back-country Pakistani family equation is simple, and to Khan's clan, there is no doubt of the worth of it as the days, years, and generations pass.

As I sit with my interpreter, I can't help but notice how much these people love their lives and each other. It's late fall, and I'm speaking to Kahn and his grown daughter Tahira in their tent in a refugee camp in Muzaffarabad, Azad Kashmir. They have retreated here in the wake of the horribly violent earthquake of three weeks ago that leveled every house in their tiny village, forty kilometers north of here. Now, winter is coming. Tahira says life in the tent camp is frustrating and their single goal is to get back to their land and rebuild, to resume their quiet lives in a place that, she says, is perfect. Here is an excerpt from a newspaper article I wrote about Khan and Tahira's family just after the quake forced them into this tent camp. "These people understand what is important in life. It is a hard-won embracing of 'what is' and a gut-level understanding that each additional breath they and their loved ones take is something for which to be enormously grateful. It's a difficult concept to grasp for a Western visitor too often caught up in soft-lifestyle frivolousness. For these simple people of the remote mountain villages, family, religion, and consistency are the necessary things—the stuff of contentment and what matters most."

I have a personal life-longing to spend a fall and winter season with a family such as Khan's, to drop my Western preoccupation with so much that doesn't matter. For these people, life is held together and makes sense because of systematic family bonds and expectations. Generations come and go, and it all works.

I watch the family's unadulterated connection and can understand the mutual serenity of the dozen families that existed together in their tiny high-elevation enclave. That serenity is shattered now, as those families have been scattered to the various tent camps of the region. These people are not happy as they get ready for the long, wet winter, eight of them living together in this dank, one-hundred-square-foot tent, but they'll stick together for the duration: No family member will abandon the rest, no matter what happens.

Where am I going with this? To compare the Western family to the Pakistani family? No. I go here: A family is a system, and it's useful to take a hard mechanical look at it as the separate entity it is, and how that entity functions within its society. Without judgment, consider the rules, the expectations; what can be questioned and what can't; who does what and why. Wherever you travel, get to know the family system of that place, thinking about the internal forces that propel it in a single direction or, in some cases, what ambiguous forces—most often in the West— tear it apart.

And so, for a Westerner, a family immersion such as this offers the opportunity to witness sharp contrast, as well as the deeply familiar, in a system that we so often take for granted. It's the ultimate outside and slightly elevated experience, and it carries the possibility of an epiphany in which a frenzied Westerner can finally understand that life is, when you get away from the superfluous, simple and precious.

CHAPTER 34

A BULL RIDER'S LIFE

This chapter is an interview I conducted with my Centratel business partner, Sam Kirkaldie. Sam is one of those lucky individuals who intuitively grasps the Systems Mindset. The interview illustrates the truth of how our lives—however and wherever they may unfold—are each a collection of individual systems. As the interview proceeds, note the myriad small processes that were part of Sam's young life in rural Montana, back in the forties and fifties. Of course, things were slower and much less complex in those days. Also notice Sam's appreciation for the life he's led.

–

Sam Kirkaldie turned seventy-six this last October.

Let's go back. Sam, his wife Bev, and three boys arrived here in Bend, Oregon, in 1976. I landed in 1978 with my wife and two children. Sam and I, acquainted since the early eighties and business partners since 2000, share the same lifestyle, entrepreneurial spirit, political viewpoint, and foundational belief that life is not complicated. Sam is physically robust (a long-distance runner), and gregarious (it seems he knows everyone in town). Before buying stock in Centratel, he was co-owner and manager of KICE Radio, the Central Oregon country and western radio station, famous for its DJs known as the "Radio Rangers." For Bend residents of thirty years ago, KICE was a communication mainstay.

In the mid-seventies there were fourteen thousand residents in Bend, most working directly or indirectly in the timber industry. Environmental activism killed off the industry in the early eighties, but the city's population has grown to 85,000 due to tourism and retirement/lifestyle transplants from all over the United States. Sam and I have watched the changes in sometimes not-so-mute fascination, and we're always ready to analyze real-life systems in action.

So, I thought it would be good to interview Sam, a true cowboy with an intriguing history, and an astute observer of life.

Part Native American, Sam was born and grew up on a cattle ranch/farm in North Central Montana on the Assiniboine Indian reservation, 120 miles north of Billings, between the Canadian border and the Missouri Breaks. With his family literally living off the land, Sam was on the ranch until he was seventeen.

Sam will tell you things are not complicated; one should work hard to be physically and mentally resilient; that it's important to be prepared and that too many people carry too much weight as they get caught up in their own heads and in things that don't matter, or they get dragged down by situations that can't be adjusted. He says it's best for youngsters to learn to stand on their own two feet at an early age. Here's the interview.

—

Sam C: In your seventy-six years, what have you learned about making a good life?

Sam K: That life is simple, but most people complicate things.

They try to carry other people's rocks around; they try to carry society's rocks. It's not healthy. You're only in control of certain segments of your life and can affect only certain things, so work on those things to the best of your ability and let everything else go. There's only so much you can do, and if you can't adjust some particular thing then don't stress over it.

When something comes up, my question is this: In one hundred years is it going to matter? Is it going to have any influence on anyone or anything? If you think about it, leaving writings behind or influencing a family member or a friend in a good way, helping people develop character and integrity, that can improve things way down the line, even a century later.

And anyway, this world is a material thing and it doesn't matter that much. I don't know if I was born with this viewpoint or if it was a product of my environment, but either way, since I was a kid, if I couldn't fix or influence something it was of little concern to me.

Sam C: Between the ages of thirteen and twenty-four, you rode bulls in rodeo competition. What about that?

Sam K: You have no control over that bull! In those days as a teenager I wasn't thinking quite so philosophically about things, but what I'd do before the ride was to get prepared: to get limbered up, warmed up, because the bull goes in all directions and the human body must be resilient or there will be injury. My last thought before release out of the chute was, "This is going to happen *real* fast, so be ready!" And then, when the gate opened, it was always way faster than I thought it was going to be!

Sam C: Of course, your last answer applies way beyond bull riding at a rodeo. Things really do move fast, don't they? How is life different from sixty years ago?

Sam K: People don't relate to each other as neighbors so much anymore. When I was a child on our farm in Montana, all the neighbors helped each other with harvests. It was a fall ritual. It was by necessity. You had to rely on neighbors. Communications were different then. People would pull up in the road beside each other in their trucks and BS, because there were no phones. If you had an event coming up, you went to the general store and put up a notice on the bulletin board, or left a note in the neighbor's mailbox. People spent more time eyeball to eyeball than they do now.

Sam C: Describe rural life in Montana in the forties and fifties.

Sam K : Our place was a combination farm/ranch. We raised cattle and horses but also had crops: wheat, barley, oats, and alfalfa for hay. We had pigs, chickens, geese, and turkeys, plus a large garden. We got electricity when I was about seven, a 32-volt wind charger that supplied lights and a small refrigerator. To stay up with the outside world, we depended on a battery-powered radio. We had no TV. The REA (Rural Electrification Administration) came to our place with commercial electric power when I was twelve.

I went to a one-room school, all eight grades in the one room, with anywhere from twelve to twenty-four students. Our house was a local gathering place, and Mom and Dad were social magnets in the community. It was usual to have anywhere from ten to forty or even fifty people (mostly aunts, uncles, and cousins who also lived in the area) at our house on summer Sundays for potluck and softball. In the cold winters, there were many evenings of cards with neighbors or just our own family members—my brother, two sisters, Mom and Dad, and my grandmother Kirkaldie.

We burned wood and coal in four different stoves in the house. There was no running water and no electric heat. It was primitive. Our main outside entertainment was gatherings at school, but on holidays we always had a number of family and friends visiting. In

the summer, we went to the bush tracks and raced our thorough-
bred horses and participated in rodeos. The local county fair was
the biggest, most looked-forward-to event of the year. Each year
there were several pow-wows, with Indian dancing and feasting.

All in all, we lived pretty well and never knew we were poor.
You learned individual responsibility early, as there were always
animals depending on your daily care. Personal independence
came with the territory: We each had our own jobs and chores to
do. I think youngsters today could gain a lot from these kinds of
experiences.

Sam C: So, what do you think of being seventy-six?

Sam K: Getting older is liberating. We have more freedom in
our actions and opinions, because we find ourselves not caring so
much what others think, so long as we're not hurting anyone. We
can be candid and know our friends will not be offended, because
they feel the same way and understand.

Sam C: Let's do stream of thought. Describe some system-
specific images that are strong memories for you right now.

Sam K: Thinking back to those days, we did have a lot of
individual systems in place. As you know, we raised the majority
of the hay and grain to feed our cows, horses, pigs, and chickens.
And on one of our fields, about sixty acres, we put several lines of
snow fence across it each fall. We positioned these lines to catch
as much drifted snow as possible during the cold winter months.
This would give the field a good moisture start in the spring, since
it was not an irrigated parcel. This would enable us to cut an early
first crop of alfalfa for hay, and the second cutting of the season
would then be run through a separator to get the seeds and provide us an additional cash crop. We would sometimes get 3,000
pounds of seed from that field, selling it on the open market for
fifty cents a pound, which was a lot of money in those days.

We also had several additional fields we irrigated by diverting the creek into a ditch we built, from about a mile upstream. We used a simple cofferdam to turn the water into our ditch, which brought the water to the uphill side of the field so we could flood-irrigate the alfalfa. These systems were inexpensive, requiring some labor but minimal investment.

The same was true of many of the ways we handled our meat and produce. When we butchered a cow, the meat we didn't eat in the first couple of days was either dried for storage or canned in quart jars by Mom, using a pressure cooker. We also did this for most of the vegetables out of our large garden. Potatoes went into the underground cellar for storage, along with carrots and root crops, which we buried in tubs of sand, keeping them fresh for months. We had an icehouse that we filled each winter by cutting large blocks of ice from a nearby reservoir. We hauled the blocks to the icehouse and put them under a couple of feet of sawdust where they would remain frozen through the entire next summer. We used the ice in our icebox to keep milk and other perishables cool, and it was also used to make ice cream. There were always a couple of blocks still in the icehouse the next winter when we prepared to fill it again for the following summer.

If we butchered a pig, the hams and bacon were brined and smoked in the smoke house. In later years, we took them to a shop in town for professional curing.

As I mentioned, the REA eventually delivered electricity to our place and this, of course, made many of our farming systems obsolete. There were even lights in the barn to replace the kerosene lanterns.

One winter before electricity came our way, we ran short of hay early in January. So Dad, my brother Joe, and my uncle Bill hauled hay from about thirty miles away for the rest of that winter. We had an old farm truck with a hayrack on it, and they pulled an additional wagon behind it to make the daily trip, hauling as much loose hay as possible. By design, the old truck did not have antifreeze in the radiator. The winter was bitter cold—often forty degrees below zero in those days—and each night they would drain the radiator and bring the battery indoors to keep as much charge in it as possible. Then, each morning they would fill the radiator with hot water and reinstall the battery so the engine would start. The truck was then left running all day rather than take the chance it might get too cold and not start again.

There were tons of small tricks and mini systems we used in those days. They were simple and reliable, enough to make our lives easier and more predictable.

Sam C: Final thoughts?

Sam K: I'm so grateful for the opportunities that have come my way. To marry a lovely, wonderful woman, have three exceptional sons, be able to make a living in the business world, and to travel extensively. It has been a great ride, and I'm looking forward to the time that remains. My gratitude for all this, and especially the friends I treasure, can't be measured.

–

So, that's Sam Kirkaldie. A great guy and my closest friend, supportive business partner, and especially, an inspiration. You can see that the Kirkaldie family's Systems Mindset had to do with maintaining relationships, perfecting routines, and in performing physical system improvements whenever possible.

In those days, did Sam and his family contemplate the human and mechanical processes around them? Yes! In every case, they knew what they wanted as an end result, constructing their individual systems with care and maintaining them carefully, all the while propelled by positive attitudes and deep gratitude. They knew how things worked, and they lived the Systems Mindset.

One more thing: Raw courage can be cultivated, and deliberately sitting oneself on an enraged bull is one way to accomplish that. Short of bull riding, what do you do in your own life to flex and strengthen the courage muscle?

CHAPTER 35

THE FABRIC OF YOUR EXISTENCE

Note: I include this chapter as a mini-meditation for those times when a quick emotional boost would be helpful. It also serves as a quick summary of the Method.

—

The world is a vast collection of individual systems. In acknowledging that, could it be that the common presumption that the world is not functioning well—that the world is a mess—is wrong?

Yes, that presumption *is* wrong, because on any given day, 99.9 percent of life's systems work perfectly. Consider the countless processes that execute with amazing efficiency: plants, animals, oceans, businesses, airplanes, bicycles, cities, whole societies, and six billion human bodies. We don't notice the exquisitely performing systems that make up our existences, so we take them for granted, never appreciating the impeccability. And the tiny number of systems we consider flawed seem that way only because they are not the way we want them to be, as they stand in stark contrast to the infinite number of perfect systems that surround them.

Yes, there is pain in the world, but as we hyperfocus on these personal, mechanical, and geopolitical systems that are not to our liking, we get swallowed up and conclude that perfection is the anomaly, imperfection the norm.

This perception is more than narrow. It's exactly backward.

Here's the crux: If you perceive the world as chaotic, your life will be chaotic. The reason for this is not because you have a bad attitude. It's purely mechanical: *If you want a machine to produce a particular end-product and you manage that machine as if it operates in a certain way, but in reality it operates in a different way, how could that machine possibly produce the end-product you want? It's as if you tried to play baseball using the rules of football: There will be chaos.*

But truly grasp that the world is not confused, that it is the opposite of that—superbly organized—and you will find your life will immediately begin to click along efficiently. There's nothing mystical about this. The world really is a remarkably sensible place, and once you align yourself with that reality you will be able to direct your life more efficiently.

As we've discussed, for some mysterious reason, systems *want* to execute perfectly, and for your personal situation you can count on an overwhelming bias toward efficiency, rather than chaos. And if your world isn't to your liking in this moment, it won't take long to get things straightened out.

I'll repeat this, too: If an outcome is not what you want it to be, it doesn't mean the system that produced that outcome is flawed. In fact, barring outside interference, that system is performing exactly as it was constructed. And so this life you live is composed of a countless number of perfect linear systems, many of which are under your control. These systems are the invisible threads that hold the fabric of your life together. If there is an outcome that doesn't suit you, you can change that outcome by making an improvement within a system, adding a system, or eliminating a system. In the typical life's rejuvenation, it's "all of the above."

And again, what of those things you can't fix because they are out of your control? Relax and move on. If you can't adjust something, don't worry about it. Metaphorically speaking, if you don't like the TV program, change the channel or turn off the set.

You are not at the mercy of mysterious conspiring forces or the swirling backwash of chaos!

Stop fire-killing and expend your time and energy on incremental system-improvement efforts that will deliver the life results you want.

CHAPTER 36

CHOOSE THE RED PILL

Not too long ago, late on a Thursday night, a friend and I watched *The Matrix* at my house. It was my fourth viewing of Larry and Andy Wachowski's film masterpiece. Watching it yet again was as profound as my first viewing.

If you are one of the seven adults in the world who hasn't seen the movie, this is your spoiler alert. *The Matrix* is best experienced cold turkey, so maybe set this chapter aside until you've seen it.

As I cued up the DVD, I glanced at the disc packaging and its brief description of the movie. The memories came back when I noticed the release date was back in 1999, just prior to my personal Systems Mindset "awakening." That insight instantly changed everything for me, and nine years later I wrote about it in *Work the System: The Simple Mechanics of Making More and Working Less.* The premise of my book is simple: that it's possible to experience a sudden and permanent change in how the world is perceived, a change that will deliver freedom and power. *The Matrix* delivers precisely the same message.

So before we began to watch the movie, I offhandedly opened a copy of *Work* to the chapter titled "Getting It" and read the quote from *The Matrix* that I used to begin the chapter.

It's Morpheus speaking, the sagacious Yoda-like character played by Laurence Fishburne.

Speaking to Neo, the protagonist in the film, played by Keanu Reeves, Morpheus said, "I'm trying to free your mind, but I can only show you the door. You're the one who has to walk through it."

For those of you who have not seen the movie and have ignored the above spoiler alert, know that the acting, special effects, and production are terrific, but it's the electrifying reality-jolt that puts it over the top as perhaps the best sci-fi movie of the past thirty years. If you watch it with a clear head and pay close attention to subtleties, it damn well makes you think. The implausible plot notwithstanding, the movie opens the door for the viewer to question up-until-now assumptions of reality.

Here is the movie's summary as noted in Wikipedia, "It depicts a dystopian future in which reality as perceived by most humans is actually a simulated reality called 'the Matrix,' created by sentient machines to subdue the human population, while their bodies' heat and electrical activity are used as an energy source. Computer programmer 'Neo' learns this truth and is drawn into a rebellion against the machines, which involves other people who have been freed from the 'dream world.'"

How does Neo learn the truth of his "dream world?" Morpheus offers him a choice, to swallow the red pill, which will show him precise reality, or take the blue pill, which will do nothing, leaving Neo to continue in his dream state and to stay ignorant of the underlying mechanical facts of his existence. Neo picks the red pill, suspecting that swallowing it could reveal a painful and irreversible hard reality. Then, in gut-churning contortion, he sees the horrible truth of his existence—that, with the exception of his new friends, virtually everyone he knows is unaware they are slaves, living in a false reality.

The message of the intense red pill/blue pill scene with

Morpheus is that Neo has put himself in a position in which he *must* choose. He can't be wishy-washy.

And again, the (not-so-subtle) message of the movie is that freedom can be gained by deliberately seeking out the down and dirty truth of how the mechanical world really operates.

Knowledge is power.

And here is the important difference between the movie's plot and the real world you and I inhabit. The Matrix's malevolent, deliberately hidden underworld exists for the sole purpose of human enslavement. In the real-life existence that you and I share, once the veil is lifted, the secret underworld offers a simple path to freedom and peace.

The movie delivers another premise: Walking away from the semi-comfortable past, never to return, could involve a certain amount of pain. This opens the question, is knowing the deeper truth worth the pain?

Will there be discomfort when you finally see the machinery of your life? Maybe some, but it will disappear fast as you begin to take control.

So we watched the movie, mesmerized. After it ended in Friday morning's wee hours, my friend left, and I, totally wired, read *Work*'s chapter 7, the one that begins with Morpheus's words. While reading, it occurred to me that back in early 1999 as I sat alone in a Saturday matinee watching *The Matrix* for the first time, it may well have been the catalyst for the systems awakening I would experience a few weeks later. Although I was mentally and physically ripe for the insight, I'm thinking it might have been this sci-fi Hollywood film that pushed me over the edge—to go a layer deeper—to finally question my fundamental take on reality, to understand for the first time that the world is not a confused mass of sights, sounds, and events, but a logical collection of linear systems.

In the beginning, as he stumbled through his everyday life, Neo felt "something is not right with the world." He carried on anyway, as we all do. Then he was offered the opportunity to see the truth of his existence, and he courageously took it.

I challenge you: If your life is not clicking along the way you think it should, dare to set aside your up-until-now menu about how you think your world operates, dig a layer deeper, and see what lies below.

Be courageous: Choose the red pill and see what happens next.

ABOUT THE AUTHOR

Sam Carpenter is the president and CEO of Centratel, the premier telephone answering service in the United States. Other businesses he founded and operates include Business Documentation Software, LLC and Work the System Consultants, LLC.

Originally from upstate New York, and an Oregonian since 1975, Sam's outside interests include mountaineering, skiing, cycling, reading, traveling, photography, and writing. *The Systems Mindset* is his second book.